GHOSTS OF BURLINGTON COUNTY

GHOSTS OF
BURLINGTON
COUNTY

HISTORICAL HAUNTINGS FROM
THE MULLICA TO THE DELAWARE

JAN LYNN BASTIEN

Published by Haunted America
A Division of The History Press
Charleston, SC 29403
www.historypress.net

Front cover: Image courtesy of Steve Hightower.
Back cover, top: Smithville Mansion, courtesy of Chas Bastien; *inset*: courtesy of the Library Company of Burlington.

Photos by author unless noted otherwise.

First published 2014

Manufactured in the United States

ISBN 978.1.60949.838.2

Library of Congress CIP data applied for.

This book is dedicated to the feral cats in Burlington County, and everywhere. These hauntingly sweet feline souls deserve our protection and compassion. Nine lives...that's a long time to be homeless.

A portion of the royalties of this book will be donated to local and national programs that help feral cats and support Trap, Neuter, Release (TNR) programs to curb the haunting tragedy of homeless cats and kittens.

CONTENTS

1

WHY DO GHOSTS HAUNT BURLINGTON COUNTY?

I'm floating down
The Mullica River oh, oh, oh
With a hold full of glass and iron
And a heart filled with love oh, oh, oh

And when the journey long
I pray to return
May the wind bring me home
—from "Mullica River" by Burlington County singer/songwriter
Heidi Winzinger

Land-wise, Burlington County is the largest county in New Jersey. Spanning from river to shining river with the mighty and historic Delaware on its western shore and the pristine Mullica on the east, more than 5,100 of its over half a million acres are water. Through it flows the Rancocas Creek and its many streams and tributaries, while sparkling lakes dot the landscape, crimson cranberry bogs bubble up in the in the pinelands every fall and other beautiful streams and waterways traverse the vast land area called Burlington County.

First settled by the Leni-Lenape Indians, Burlington County is steeped with early American history and folklore. The American Revolution was fought here, the Underground Railroad ran through here and it has been home to the likes of pirates, patriots and the infamous Jersey Devil. From the writings on the cell walls at the Burlington County Prison Museum in Mount

The serene waters of the Mullica River are beautiful to look at and are a peaceful resting place for pirates of long ago.

Holly to the footprints of the Jersey Devil in the pinelands, many have left their imprint in Burlington County, and some may have never left at all.

In the 1670s, Quakers arrived here seeking religious freedom. Persecuted in England for refusing to bear arms, they sought a new, peaceful land and found it in West Jersey. Today, their historic meetinghouses are in many Burlington County towns, and several of them are still in use, by both current parishioners and some friendly ghosts. While the Quakers were peaceful and spiritual people, though not especially open to paranormal theories, it cannot be denied that many of their historic houses of worship are also very spiritual, and not just in the divine sense. Many have been investigated by professional paranormal investigators and have been found to be definitely haunted. The Mount Holly Quaker Meeting House was found to be haunted with both residual and interactive spirit activity. Arney's Mount Meeting House, in Springfield Township, has spirit activity in its burial grounds, which predate the meetinghouse itself. Actually, both are haunted. Friendly ghosts have also been discovered in the Coopertown Meeting House in Edgewater Park. During an investigation there, South Jersey Ghost Research (SJGR) investigators saw an apparition enter the building from the cemetery side and later, after observing a shadow move at the front of the building, captured a photo that looks like a hooded monk praying.

In contrast to the peacefulness of the Quakers, pirate activity thrived along the county's rivers and even up the Rancocas Creek. One British general labeled the Mullica River a "nest of pirate activity" as the likes of Captain Kidd, Captain John VanSant and Joe Mulliner sailed those pineland waters, hiding out in the many necks and coves tucked into the coastline and robbing British merchant vessels during the American Revolution. Mulliner was known as much for his partying as his pirating, a kind of local celebrity who liked to crash parties in the pineland areas of southeastern Burlington County and across the river in Atlantic County, stealing pretty women from their partners and dancing with the ladies as their escorts stewed on the sidelines. But his cavalier cavorting led to his demise one night in 1781 as one of these disgruntled boyfriends went to the local authorities while the dancing pirate cut the rug with his girlfriend. Captain Baylor of the local militia, who had been waiting for his chance to capture Mulliner, rounded up a posse and headed to the party. They got Mulliner and jailed him. He was tried in Burlington City, where he was found guilty of treason and was hanged the very same day. Buried in the Jersey pinelands, it is said that his booming laughter can be heard along the banks of the Mullica, and some have even reported seeing his ghost

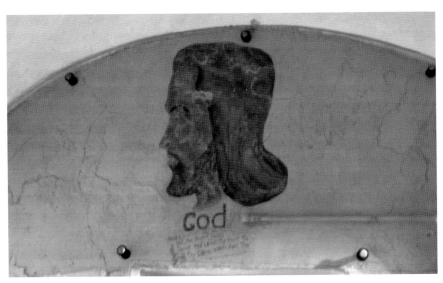

Dead inmates speak to us through their graffiti on the walls of the Burlington County Prison Museum. *Photo by Larry Tigar.*

there, brandishing pistols to protect his treasures, which are claimed to be buried along the banks of that sparkling river.

The notorious Blackbeard may have sailed the Mullica, but he was more well known on the Delaware River. Born Edward Teach in Bristol, England, in the 1680s, he was one of the fiercest pirates who ever lived. He got his name from his very black beard, which he often braided with ribbons and decorated with smoking fuses. He was aware of his ominous appearance and how it intimidated his foes. But it didn't scare the ladies, as it is said he had more wives than Henry VIII. He reportedly had a girlfriend in Burlington and a wife in Marcus Hook, Pennsylvania, and the Delaware would provide an easy commute between their doorsteps. His journeys took him up and down the East Coast, and he often stocked up on food for his voyages at a store in Burlington before setting sail.

Blackbeard reportedly buried a treasure in Burlington City, at the foot of Wood Street under a huge walnut tree, whose stump remained there until 1875. Whenever Blackbeard buried treasure, he summoned a volunteer to come ashore to guard it. Then, he would routinely kill him and bury the fool with the treasure, as his secret was better kept with a dead man. He also liked to bury the volunteer standing upright on top of the treasure, to scare anyone trying to rob it. At the Burlington treasure site, a Spaniard on board volunteered to stand guard. Blackbeard shot him and, for some reason, also shot the ship's dog and buried him along with the Spaniard and the treasure.

One legend has it that Blackbeard returned for the treasure one stormy night; however, through lightning flashes, he observed a coven of witches dancing around the spot, and he never returned again. But there were many reports through the years that residents of Wood Street saw a black dog, which would just fade away if approached, sitting where the tree was.

Water attracts more than pirates; paranormal researchers know it carries energy for spirits to manifest. It is one possible reason that this water-rich county harbors as many spirits as it does. The industrial villages of Smithville and Roebling, the company towns of Pemberton and Riverside and the mills in Mount Holly were all built near and powered by water. So while the water powered industry and helped these communities move forward, it also tends to let the past remain with us. The water that powered mills and factories today conducts energy for the souls of earthbound spirits to interact with us.

Any place with a lot of history tends to have a lot of ghosts. It just makes sense—there is more material! But if the history has an emotional charge to it, there is even more of a chance the area will be haunted. Wars,

The mighty Delaware River in Burlington City is where Blackbeard buried his treasure.

imprisonment, escape from captivity, sickness and other tragedies often leave more traces of spirit activity on a place. Ghosts seem to latch on to the emotional energy of others, but more often, people who have died during emotional turmoil have a harder time crossing over. They often tend to linger near their last place on earth, maybe even their favorite place, or near a loved one. There are numerous reasons why a spirit has not or cannot cross over, and an unreconciled life of turmoil is certainly one of them.

In the center of Burlington County is a large military installation. Formerly distinct, Fort Dix and Maguire Air Force Base have recently been joined together, along with nearby Lakehurst Naval Base, to form Joint Base Maguire-Dix-Lakehurst, or JBMDL. JBMDL covers forty-two thousand contiguous acres, mostly in the New Jersey Pine Barrens. Due to that fact, it is not that surprising that many soldiers stationed there as far back as World War II have reported sightings of the Jersey Devil on the grounds. Many of these sightings have been in the vicinity where Walson Army Hospital now stands.

Walson was opened on Fort Dix on the ides of March in 1960. Once, its five hundred beds were filled to capacity with soldiers returning from

Vietnam and soldiers' wives having babies there. As if just being a military hospital wasn't enough, it had a psychiatric ward on the seventh floor and a morgue in the basement—fertile ground for hauntings! Five years after Walson opened, a "ghost" even died there! In July 1965, Constance Bennett, who was married to U.S. Air Force brigadier general John Coulter, died of a cerebral hemorrhage in Walson. Ms. Bennett was an actress and well known for her role as a female ghost—the wife of Topper, played by Carey Grant—in the 1950s movie *Topper*, which later spawned the TV sitcom of the same name.

But the ghostly activity at Walson is not just made for TV. From orbs floating around its hallways to unexplained temperature fluctuations and actual sightings of apparitions, this location has been rife with ghost stories since it opened. A 2008 article titled "America's Haunted Army," posted on the army's official website, told of reports of eerie happenings, especially in the basement morgue and in the psychiatric ward. One medical group staffer reported that after security checks were done, they would find doors to the pharmacy entrance unlocked, even though they were locked up tight just an hour earlier. Windows opened by themselves, and lights would flicker and turn off and on by themselves. In the morgue, they heard the sound of a grown man crying.[1] There are also many stories about babies crying and a ghostly orderly mopping the floor in the maternity ward. The bucket and mop are always found in the corner, dry from years of neglect, but the floor has been seen to be wet, freshly mopped, with footprints across it.

South Jersey Ghost Research (SJGR) had finally received permission from the military to conduct a professional paranormal investigation at the army hospital in 2001, but after 9/11 occurred and security at the base was significantly increased, the investigation was canceled. And now we might never have that scientific evidence about what is causing the ghostly activity, as Walson is shuttered and prepared for demolition. Will the weary ghosts finally take some liberty?

As we uncover the history of more of the haunted buildings that stand between these two great rivers, we'll try to determine what might have gone on that's causing paranormal activity today. While it is often not possible to pinpoint exactly who is haunting a building, knowing something about prior events, major characters and the historical significance of a building can give us clues and some insight about what is going on today. Information from interviews with people who have experienced the activity—professional paranormal researchers, caretakers, curators and directors—has been very helpful in trying to theorize about what can be going on there.

Now that the Walson Army Hospital is shuttered and ready for demolition, where will the ghosts go? *Photo by Chas Bastien.*

"Mount Holly should have been named Mount Haunted!" quipped SJGR assistant director Maureen Carroll during a 2013 presentation about this haunted county's historic and ghostly county seat. We will tag along with SJGR, the Delaware Valley's most experienced, professional paranormal investigation team, as they explore the Mount Holly Elks and the Burlington County Lyceum of History and Natural Sciences. (Interestingly, when most paranormal researchers investigate a historic building, they often purposely do not research any of the building's history prior to the investigation so that their findings are not tainted by preassumed happenings.)

Many of the ghosts we will meet here have been through emotional turmoil, live near water or died a sudden, unexpected death. Some have experienced more than one of these conditions, and some don't fall into any of these categories but are still here. Some are curious to see who is in their home and how they are taking care of it; some might have died unexpectedly and don't even realize they are dead.

Some might be just as interested in meeting you as you are to meet them, so let's get to know some of the ghosts of Burlington County.

2

WHEREVER AN ELK MAY ROAM

We're all like detectives in life. There's something at the end of the trail that we're all looking for.
—David Lynch, American filmmaker

On June 30, 2012, we were three days from the full Mother's Moon, a moon that folklore tells us celebrates the variety of life and the glory of each stage: birth, reproduction and death. The summer solstice had just passed and the air was hot, cloaking us with dense humidity, as the area had just suffered through its third day of the year's second heat wave. The previous night had produced severe thunderstorms for Mount Holly, and in an area just thirty miles south, a "derecho" had ripped through portions of rural South Jersey, uprooting large trees and crushing houses, barns and other buildings in one of the most destructive storms in the history of the area, pre–Superstorm Sandy. But on this night, the sky was clear over Mount Holly, and the brilliant moon seemed to watch us in anticipation as we made our way to meet the South Jersey Ghost Research (SJGR) investigators and see what spirits were raising suspicions at the Mount Holly Elks Lodge #848.

Mike O'Connor, the lodge's house committee chairman, met us at the bar and told us that some members had heard footsteps, especially on the third floor. As we waited for SJGR's arrival, Mike filled us in on the history of the Mount Holly Elks. The building, sitting at 116 High Street in Mount Holly's historic district, was originally the home and law office of John R. Slack, built circa 1856. The stately residence had boasted four bedrooms, a parlor, a library, a kitchen, a dining room and a rear porch. There are six marble fireplaces; two solid oak entry doors that welcome guests through the front entrance; beautiful cornice work throughout; elaborate lighting fixtures; and high, plastered walls and ceilings, many graced with ornate, plaster medallions.

The bar, where we sat, was a new addition to the building from the 1950s. Before the addition, the parlor had French doors that opened to a garden in the back. When the building became an Elks Lodge in 1903, ladies congregated there, waiting for their husbands to bring them drinks, as most of the lodge was off-limits to women.

More than Elks roam the Mount Holly Elks Lodge.

The Mount Holly Lodge was officially instituted a Benevolent and Protective Order of Elks on April 23, 1903, with an induction ceremony that was held farther down High Street at the Mount Holly Opera House, a building that, unfortunately, no longer exists, a casualty of urban renewal. That evening, 255 men were inducted as charter members of the Mount Holly Lodge. Because it was such a large number, 2 principal candidates received the ceremonious initiation on behalf of the all the inductees. Those 2 men were Brother Blanchard White and Brother Ellis Parker Sr., both prominent figures in Mount Holly at the time.

Ellis Parker, in fact, was quite a legend, and not only in Mount Holly. Known as America's Sherlock Holmes, Ellis Parker was Burlington County's first chief of detectives. He solved hundreds of murder cases and thousands of other crimes, obtaining signed confessions in more than half of them.

Born a Quaker in nearby Wrightstown, New Jersey, in 1871, young Parker aspired to be a musician. But when somebody stole his horse and wagon with his fiddle in it, he investigated the crime himself. After he found the horse and other belongings, his interest began to turn to law enforcement and investigations. As his career progressed, Ellis Parker became so well known that law enforcement investigators from all over the United States and even other countries sought his help. But sadly, he died disgraced and incarcerated because he overstepped his bounds as a law enforcement official.

It was the famous Lindbergh baby case that brought down the super sleuth. He was brought into the case late, and perhaps for that reason, he was a little miffed and became overzealous. In 1936, just as Bruno Hauptmann was scheduled to be executed for the crime, Parker came forward with a confession from another man, Paul Wendell, a disbarred Trenton attorney. Believing Hauptmann to be innocent, Parker and his son, Detective Ellis Parker Jr., kidnapped Wendell and forced him into a confession. Hauptmann's execution was delayed several days, but Wendell's forced confession was overturned. Parker and his son were accused of kidnapping and torturing Wendell to get his confession and were convicted and sentenced to prison, six years for Parker Sr. and three for his son.

Ellis Parker Sr. died on February 5, 1940, in the federal penitentiary in Lewisberg, Pennsylvania. His son was at his bedside, and his family was racing down icy Pennsylvania roads to try to get to him to say goodbye. They didn't make it in time. Alone and disgraced after a brilliant career as one of America's finest detectives, he left this world just as President Roosevelt was about to pardon him and restore his dignity. On February 5, 1940, the *Camden Courier Post* wrote:

Parker died in the Penitentiary, as the wheels of Federal pardon were grinding towards a Presidential pardon. Had Parker lived another week, he would have been back home in his beloved Mount Holly—a free man, with all of his civil rights restored. The man whom thousands called the "greatest detective in the world" died at 3:55 a.m., and even then, the U.S. mails were carrying documents to Judge William Clark, preparatory to an executive pardon from President Roosevelt.[2]

While alive, Parker had enjoyed spending much of his free time at the Mount Holly Elks Lodge #848. He lived barely a block away on the other side of the street at 215 High Street, and his office was at the stately Burlington County Courthouse on High Street, two doors down from the Elks. So if he wasn't working on a case or at home, he could often be found at the Elks. In fact, Parker's arrest came on June 3, 1936, while he sat with a group of friends on the porch of the Mount Holly Elks club,[3] so this was one of the last places he spent time in Mount Holly. Has he returned there after death to remain in a happier time when he hung out at the bar with his contemporaries, who recognized him as one of the greatest detectives who ever lived? Many believe they have seen him in the second-floor window, looking down on High Street.

SJGR investigators arrived at about 9:30 p.m., toting bags and cases of equipment. The team of seven—including SJGR director Dave Juliano—all dressed in black, unpacked the equipment and laid it out on the table in the first-floor meeting room. Team members checked each piece of inventory to be sure all was charged and working properly to accurately record their findings. Some of the high-tech ghost-hunting tools SJGR packed to detect paranormal activity at the Mount Holly Elks lodge were digital voice recorders to capture possible EVPs (electronic voice phenomena), should any spirits want to communicate; EMF (electromagnetic field) meters to measure electromagnetic fluctuations (ghost hunters theorize that spirits have the ability to manipulate EMFs and that fluctuations, therefore, could indicate ghosts are present); a swanky new piece of equipment called an ATDD meter, which is a multipurpose tool that measures EMFs and ambient temperature and helps detect shadows; a laser grid scope, a device that will shoot a bunch of green dots in a grid on a wall to help detect shadows; infrared cameras; infrared light extenders; and full-spectrum HD video cameras.

Juliano asked Mike about the members still at the bar in the back and how long they would be there. Mike said not to worry about them, they would not disturb the investigators. Dave was concerned that their voices could affect SJGR's findings. Mike said that the noises and footsteps were heard on the third floor, anyway. "Just because that's where they were heard, doesn't mean that's where they are coming from," explained Juliano. Mike said the bar was about ready to close, so it would not hamper the investigation. Mike then showed the team around the building.

On the second floor, there was a large lodge meeting room, with chairs surrounding the perimeter, an altar and special chairs for officers. On the way into this room, we first went through the "Ante-Room," whose wall is adorned with gold-plated name tags of all deceased members. Among them is that of Ellis H. Parker Sr., dated February 4, 1940. There was also a large billiards room in the front of the second floor and then the stairway to the third floor.

Another interesting room on the second floor was a barroom the team nicknamed "the speakeasy" because it was used during Prohibition. You could tell some wild times were probably had in the room during the Roaring Twenties, with the slot machine that can flip behind the wall and a bar whose stash could disappear down a dumbwaiter should a visit be paid by Mount Holly's finest. This room would definitely be a place in which partying ghosts might like to hang out! I could almost hear the glasses clinking and music playing.

The third floor was hot—ninety-six degrees. A caretaker called this room home in the late 1960s and early '70s. Today, it is just used for storage. But Mike told us that footsteps are often heard coming from this floor, when they know nobody is up here. Also, recently some members reported smelling cigarette smoke, and nobody has smoked up here in decades.

The investigation officially got underway at 10:30 p.m., and as Mike had promised, the bar downstairs was closed. It was only Brother Elk Mike O'Connor and those involved with the investigation who remained in the historic building. Juliano split his team into two groups, and one started up to the third floor while the other checked out the second floor first.

The heat was close to unbearable on the third floor that night, but it didn't seem to thwart any spirit activity. Investigators Mike Zahn, Kim Pietrzak and Chris Bygrave took that floor on first, and Dave joined them. Kim saw a shadow in the doorway entrance to the front room up there, and as Mike entered the room, he heard the floor creak next to him. Then he and Dave both heard a loud bang behind them. Mike felt somebody walk past him into the main room. When they set up their EVP sensors, he asked if somebody there wished to communicate with them. A voice on the EVP recorder responded "boy." They knew they were not alone.

In his case notes, Zahn wrote that he felt "3 young kids (7yr–10yr old) playing in the main room…I saw a small, short shadow move through the doorway into the main room." A few minutes later, he saw another small, short shadow move past the door in the hallway. "I got the impression of young kids playing hide-and-seek around us." He also heard footsteps in the bathroom, and they recorded an EVP that sounded like a young girl saying, "Please catch me." Chris saw a shadow about three and a half feet tall move around a Christmas tree stored in the corner. Then, about ten minutes later, in the intense heat of the attic, Chris felt cold and shivered, a sensation lasting about five seconds, at a time when both Chris and Mike recorded feeling the presence of three children—"young souls," as Bygrave documented—playing like it was a game of hide-and-seek.

Kim Pietrzak sensed the children playing, also, and asked what their names were. She got an EVP response saying "Steve." She smelled a strong cigar smell around her soon after that. Juliano explained to his investigators that there are many ways the spirits can communicate with them. Right after that, they got another EVP recording that said "no." Was that directed at the investigators, or was someone reprimanding the children—or the cigar smoker?

"I also got the impression of an older gentleman dressed in a suit and tie that was hiding in the small room to the right of the top of the stairs. I felt as though he was hiding from the authorities and was very anxious and nervous, not willing to communicate with anyone at all. He felt more like a residual energy, compared to the children that felt like intelligent energies trying to interact with us," Zahn continued in his notes about his third-floor investigation.

The glass clinking I anticipated when first seeing the "speakeasy" actually materialized when Zahn and Pietrzak went to investigate the second floor. "I heard the sound of two glasses or a bottle and glass clang together from behind the bar in the speakeasy," recorded Zahn at 12:33 a.m. He continued, "While I was behind the bar asking for communication, I felt as though I got poked in the eye. I asked if the poke in the eye meant that I wasn't welcome behind the bar, and felt an even harder poke in the same eye. It was hard enough to make me see stars in that eye." An EVP recording, taken a few minutes later, advised Mike, "Just walk away," and then he felt a hand grab his right shoulder.

So Mike decided to switch gears, trying some role playing with the spirits in the speakeasy to evoke communication. Asking the "bartender" if he had "change for a twenty," they immediately captured an EVP saying "Yes."

About ten minutes later, as Kim and I watched a shadow move through the laser grid in an area just above the slot machines, an EVP was captured that said, "Restrain me." A few minutes after that, another EVP was captured saying, "Top me off again." Could it be that some spirits were just out for a Saturday night drink, unconcerned with the ghost hunters' presence, while others were quite annoyed about it?

Meanwhile, investigators Mark McKinny, Mandy McCaw and Kathy Smith were busy in the second-floor meeting room. Mark felt like somebody was standing over him as he sat on the left side of the room near the bronze Elk head, and then he heard a whisper in his left ear. Mandy immediately felt the presence of someone whose name came across to her as "Tom," and she felt he was trying to show her where his seat was in the meeting room. But then, a stronger presence made her feel overwhelmingly unwelcome in there, so she left and went to the third floor, where she encountered an elderly gentleman with white hair, pacing in the hallway.

Later, McKinney joined her and Kathy Smith on the third floor, and they used the ATDD to communicate with the spirits. The ATDD alarmed "red" several times, indicating a temperature fluctuation. Since it was so unbearably hot up there, they wanted to be sure, and so they reset the meter to validate its accuracy. And then Mandy said to the possible spirit presence, "If someone is up here, could you please make another light come on or flash one of the red lights?" Within seconds, another red light lit up on the ATDD. She responded, "Is that confirmation you are here?" The red light flashed. Investigator McKinney asked the apparent spirit, "Can you do it again?" and within seconds, it flashed again. Investigator Smith felt that this spirit had held the position of sergeant-at-arms in the Elks and asked him to confirm, and the ATDD again flashed. Smith also "received the year 1933" and an older man with white hair and a mustache as a psychic impression.

"Be quiet!" an EVP admonished Zahn at around 11:30 p.m. as he began to set up his equipment in the second-floor meeting room in preparation for his team to investigate there. These spirits are tough and stern and maybe a little reluctant to change for newcomers. The Mount Holly Elks Lodge was one of the last to allow women to join its ranks, and Mandy McCaw was not the only female investigator who was made to feel unwelcome in its meeting room. Investigator Kim Pietrzak stated in her case notes, "Upon entering the room, I felt as though I had to leave, like I wasn't welcomed." But she persevered, going back a second time after taking a break, and entered with Zahn. At 12:24 a.m., she recorded that as she and Zahn entered the room, "we both saw a full-bodied apparition of a very tall thin man standing next to the flag pole. This apparition turned, then walked away and disappeared."

Later, McCaw and McKinney went back to the meeting room to investigate again. They both sensed a spirit in there and, using the ATDD again, tried to determine the spirit's age and when he was a member. Asking the spirit to manipulate the lights on the meter as they asked a series of questions, the spirit told them he was definitely a member of the Elks in the 1990s, and at that time, he was younger than sixty years old. This was all ascertained after a series of a dozen questions, asking the spirit to respond by flashing the lights. At 12:47 a.m., McCaw documented, "I get the impression he is using up his energy and communicating with us via the ATDD is getting more difficult for him."

"The Elks Lodge is teeming with activity, most of which appears to be of an intelligent nature," summed up investigator Pietrzak.

Zahn also concluded, "During the investigation, I encountered residual energies as well as intelligent energies. I don't feel as though there are any negative or malevolent energies present at this location…all the energies I encountered were benevolent or just as curious about us as we were of them." I guess he forgave the one that poked him in the eye!

Could one of these spirits be the ghost of Ellis Parker? Investigator Smith got the impression of the year 1933, when Parker would have been an active member, but was that him? Some saw a man with a mustache, and old photos of Parker show him sporting a 'stache. And the impression of the man in a suit and tie trying to avoid authorities could definitely point to Ellis Parker, as this great American sleuth spent much of his time at the Elks and was even arrested there. As for the spirits in the speakeasy, it's hard to say if they were just some Prohibition-breaking revelers or someone noteworthy, such as Parker. He was known to smoke a pipe but how about a cigar, or was that really a cigar that Investigator Pietrzak smelled? And who were the children? Did they belong to a former caretaker, or were they part of Attorney Slack's family?

The truth is there are apparently several spirits haunting the Mount Holly Elks Lodge, and the trouble with paranormal investigations is that it is often much easier to detect spirits than to determine whose spirits they are, especially in a lodge that has been home to the Elks for over one hundred years and home to a family prior to that. The evidence is clear that the footsteps members hear are paranormal manifestations. But is Parker there? While it appears likely, it would take a good detective to know for sure.

3
WHO'S HOME AT THE BARCLAY HAINES HOMESTEAD?

Where we love is home—home that our feet may leave, but not our hearts.
—Oliver Wendell Holmes Sr., American poet and writer

Before European settlers invaded Burlington County and the area where Hainesport now stands, the Leni-Lenape Indians inhabited this land along the Rancocas Creek. They called the creek the Ankokus, and it provided them with food and irrigation for their crops. They called this fertile land Sandhickney. By the mid-1700s, European settlers pretty much had claimed Sandhickney for their own, leaving barely a ghost of a memory of the Native American population that had lived here for about ten thousand years previously.

Many Quaker families settled this area, including Richard and Margaret Haines, who sailed from Northamptonshire, England, in 1682. Margaret gave birth to a son, Joseph, mid-trip. They were headed for religious freedom and a land grant of about 1,700 acres, which covered part of present-day Mount Laurel. When Joseph got older, he purchased land that covered several hundred acres in the village of Long Bridge. The village was so named because there was a long wooden toll bridge crossing the Rancocas on Philadelphia Road, a roadway that went from Mount Holly to Moorestown and today is known as Marne Highway, or County Road 537. In 1778, this bridge was dismantled by area colonists to delay the advance of British troops from Philadelphia, led by British commander in chief Sir Henry Clinton, whose secretary recorded the incident in this manner:

At a small distance from… [Mount Holly] *a bridge was broken down by the rebels which, when our people were repairing, were fired upon by those villains from a house, two of which were taken prisoners, three killed and the other two ran into the cellar and fastened it so we were obliged to burn the house and consume them in it.*[4]

Years later, Barclay Haines, a sixth-generation Haines, born in Evesham Township, went to Philadelphia to make his fortune as a contractor. He was a prominent Lumberton landowner in 1847, when he bought 311 acres on the south branch of the Rancocas in Long Bridge. He built a wharf and a beautiful Victorian home on the property, which he called "the Homestead." He and his wife, Lydia, raised four children there: Albert, Edwin, Allen and Mary. Barclay and Lydia lived at the Homestead the rest of their days, until 1881 for him and 1907 for her.

The Rancocas was a major waterway during Barclay Haines's time. Every day you could hear the whistles of steamboats blasting as the ships carried their freight and passengers back and forth between Haines's port

Barclay Haines's Homestead stands steadfast today and is home to more than earthly residents.

and Philadelphia. Ladies would wait for the arrival of the steamships in a gazebo at the edge of the water, which Haines provided for this purpose. Barclay Haines owned a steamboat himself, which he christened *The Barclay*, and used it to transport lumber and coal to Philadelphia.

At Haines's port, stagecoaches dropped off passengers, and freight wagons unloaded their cargo as this bustling headquarters for steamer navigation expanded on the Rancocas. Imagine the crowds and the excitement of this busy little port. Soon the village of Long Bridge became known as Haines' Port, and in 1850, the name of this town, which had become a transportation hub for the entire area, was officially changed to Hainesport, as it is still known today.

In 1875, Mary Haines married Dr. William Conrad Parry in the formal gardens of her family's home, and four years later, they moved in with her parents. The beautiful home and gardens on the sloping bank of the Rancocas became their home for the rest of their lives, and they raised three children there: Lydia, Edda and William. Edda died tragically at eighteen at the home from appendicitis. When Mrs. Haines died in 1907, her son-in-law, who had been managing the homestead after the death of Barclay, took over as its new master. He died four years later, and his wife passed in 1929. They are both buried in the Mount Holly Friends Cemetery.

Possession of the Homestead then passed to Lydia "Lil" Middleton Parry, their spinster daughter. There are reports of others who might have shared the Homestead with Lil, including her nephew William; his wife, Julia; their daughter, Judith; another nephew, Bob; his wife, Helen; and a Mrs. Marion Endress Brosius and a Mr. Theodore Rodman. When Lil died in 1960, she left the Homestead to her favorite nephew, William Haines Parry.

Robert Winzinger, a farmer from Springfield Township, bought the stately mansion from William Haines Parry, as at the time of his inheritance of the Homestead, Parry had accepted employment in Florida. So today, the Barclay Haines Homestead is for the first time in the loving hands of a family not part of Barclay Haines's lineage—the Winzingers. The port of Barclay Haines is long gone now, and all that remains of its passenger docks and freight wharves are a few broken pilings in the creek. It is said that the remains of Barclay rest in a little cove between the railroad bridge and the house. The Winzingers have reconstructed Barclay Haines's gazebo alongside the Rancocas, but ships no longer stop here as the Rancocas is not as deep as it was back then and is no longer navigated by large passenger and cargo ships headed to Philadelphia.

Today, a new gazebo stands alongside the Rancocas Creek, where long ago passengers waited to board a steamship to Philadelphia.

Robert Winzinger came from humble beginnings, raised by a single mother on a farm off Jacksonville Road in Springfield Township. When he and his young wife, JoAnn, a graduate of St. Mary's in Burlington, purchased the Homestead, their first child, Audrey, was on the way. Robert and JoAnn Winzinger raised six children at the Barclay Haines Homestead while working hard to build their business, Winzinger Incorporated, which has served the construction, demolition and land improvement industries for over forty years. Their company office building was built right next door to the mansion, on the bank of the Rancocas.

The Winzingers' six children are Audrey, Robin, Heidi, Linda, Phil and Robert Jr. ("R.T." to his siblings). Robin and Heidi remember their childhood years at the Homestead. "The upstairs was closed off; somebody who lived here before had polio, so they closed off the stairs. The kitchen sink had a pump, and there was a freezer in the back. There were delivery men for all types of food back then, and Mom filled it up because she didn't like to cook," recalls Heidi.

"Mom rarely cooked anything that didn't come in a box," laughed Robin, who, maybe because of this, grew up to become a chef and now owns the popular Robins Nest Restaurant in Mount Holly. But the shortcomings in the kitchen did not stop JoAnn Winzinger from creating a fabulously unique home for her family, using many items obtained through the family demolition business. Mantels and doors, shutters, hardware, flooring, white milk glass and many artifacts from old buildings can be found in the old Barclay Haines Homestead. While Winzinger Incorporated is contracted to destroy buildings, JoAnn sometimes finds it difficult to say goodbye to these beautiful, historic places and brings these memories home to live with her. Her love of the past and the good quality and craftsmanship of these antique furnishings are found throughout her home. And maybe the energy of some of these old places lives on in the intriguing décor that JoAnn Winzinger has created here in the old Barclay Haines Homestead.

If you have toured the Winzinger estate, which you may have done on a local holiday house tour, you can't help but think how much fun it must have been to grow up here as a child. Staircases and closed-off areas produced hiding places throughout the home. The girls' bedrooms are upstairs, and each daughter had a different room with a unique theme. They are decorated with gingerbread woodwork from a demolition site and girly lace curtains. There are nooks, crannies, cutouts and coves; one room has a trundle bed and the other a canopy bed. SJGR investigated this home twice, and Director Dave Juliano noted, "It's like a time capsule. These bedrooms are preserved like the young daughters still live here. The dolls and other little girl decorations are in place, like they never grew up and moved out."

As if the bedrooms and back staircases weren't enough fun, the Winzingers added a pool room—no, not a billiards room, a full swimming pool room! "The pool building is a big combination of lots of things. The balconies that overlook the building as you come out of the old part of the house are columns from the train station in London. But the rest of the building is all sorts of building materials that Mom collected from various jobs all over the place," explained Heidi.

Having grown up on the banks of the Rancocas, Heidi and Robin can relate numerous childhood memories of kids drowning in the swift waters of the creek right near their home. "We would sit by the window and watch them dredge the creek for their bodies," Heidi remembered. Maybe one reason for the pool was to prevent the Winzinger children and playmates from being one of those ill-fated children who took to the swift waters of the Rancocas.

While they shared the adventure of growing up in Haines's old Homestead, Heidi and Robin both have ghost stories to tell that they didn't share with each other at the time, so neither knew the fright the other had experienced.

One was a ghost they both refer to as the "Blue Ghost." He first came to Robin shortly after their grandfather died from a heart attack in the house and was taken out in a stretcher, with her grandmother screaming, "George! George!" At first, Robin thought her Blue Ghost had something to do with this, but later she discounted any link between the Blue Ghost and her grandfather's death.

"I distinctly remember waking up one night and seeing a blue, illuminated figure in my room," recalled Robin. "It was a man in army clothes, like Civil War–type. He was young and handsome, probably in his late 20s." Robin lay in her bed, paralyzed with fear. She kept this a secret from the rest of her family because she thought nobody would believe her. He never came again, but to this day, Robin contends, "He was very real. He was definitely there and very blue, very illuminated and very handsome." Robin also often heard heavy footsteps on the stairs, like a soldier marching.

Years later, the Blue Ghost appeared to Heidi. The night of his visit, she was sleeping in the front bedroom, which faces Marne Highway. "I was in bed, and I saw a handsome soldier with an illuminated, blue aura. He just stood there staring at me. I couldn't move, so I just lay there and then I squeezed my eyes shut." Today, after sharing these experiences, Heidi and Robin are both positive that they saw the same ghost.

Robin and Heidi would often hear footsteps on the uncarpeted stairway between the landing and Audrey's room. They would assume it was their mother coming up the steps, but it never was. No person was coming up the steps, but the footsteps were often heard at night while they lay in their beds, listening, wondering. Their mother often moved them from room to room if they mentioned they were frightened. Sometimes they would sleep together in the same room—safety in numbers against the spirits.

Can you remember one house where you and all your friends wanted to hang out while growing up? Not surprisingly, the Winzinger mansion was this type of house, and Heidi's best friend, Nancy, spent a lot of time there during their youth. As young girls, Nancy and Heidi both had very long hair. One time, when Nancy was staying over, she was brushing her long tresses in the hallway mirror near Heidi's third-floor bedroom with the trundle bed. As she turned her head and flipped her hair to the other side, she saw the Blue Ghost in Heidi's bedroom. It was the same handsome young man with the blue, illuminating glow. Frightened, Nancy told Robin what had happened, and for the first time, Robin knew she was not the only one who had seen the Blue Ghost. Now, there were three independent accounts of his presence at the old Barclay Haines Homestead. They are positive they all saw the same ghost.

Heidi remembered a hot summer day when she was a teenager; it was very warm in the house. She was in her bedroom, shaving her legs on her bed. Suddenly, the room became icy cold. She had to stop shaving because her legs became covered with goose bumps it was so cold in her room. "Something was in the room with me," Heidi recalled. "I felt something take hold of my leg, and I ran out of the room, hyperventilating! I didn't go back all night. It scared me to death." While Heidi only felt this entity and didn't see anything this time, this happened in the same room that the Blue Ghost appeared to Nancy.

Another time, Heidi was sleeping in the back addition of the home, where her brother Phil often slept. Their dog, Duke, a brindle boxer, was sleeping on the floor next to the bed. Heidi was awakened by Duke's growling. The moon was shining through the window, illuminating the room, and Duke, still growling, sat up alertly with his ears up; something was going on. Heidi lay quietly and motionless in the bed and then watched as a black blur floated through the room. "Duke went crazy. It was like an energy field; I couldn't see an image. It just went across the room and then it was gone."

While JoAnn doesn't often have time to talk about or bother with ghosts in her house, she has said that she has felt her bed move for no apparent reason and has heard voices coming from a closed-off staircase. Robin and Heidi remember their mom would sometimes hear the piano playing and somebody singing when nobody was in the piano room at all.

Heidi got to know Dave Juliano and South Jersey Ghost Research when SJGR participated in Mount Holly's annual Witches Ball event and Heidi was an event coordinator. SJGR expressed interest in investigating the old Homestead, and Heidi arranged for researchers to come to her parents' home and see if maybe they could lend validity to some of the "disturbances" she had experienced there as a child.

SJGR investigated the Winzingers' home on the evening of July 22, 2000, and again on September 29, 2001. Some of their findings seem to be in direct correlation to the experiences Robin and Heidi report. They all experienced an entity on the staircase where the girls had frequently heard footsteps, and it felt like something was following them. Some investigators even reported feeling like they were being pushed from behind. Positive orbs were captured on the staircases and the landings.

"When we went back the second time, because of these experiences on the staircase, we played tricks on the new investigators," laughed Juliano. "Once we got upstairs, we pretended we left some equipment downstairs and asked them to go get it. Then we just kind of watched and laughed as they felt the thing push them down the stairs. We knew it was going to happen, and it was fun to watch their reaction."

SJGR also recorded positive orbs in the dining room, in the pool area and throughout the girls' bedrooms. Positive orbs were also captured throughout the piano room, including around the piano, and investigator John McDougall felt something pull his ear while he stood near the piano. The same paranormal virtuoso that JoAnn heard playing, maybe?

In the room in which Nancy saw the Blue Ghost and Heidi felt the presence while shaving, investigator Pam Porado felt something near her, and when a photo was snapped, a positive orb was captured. Juliano saw a dark figure go into one of the third-floor bedrooms, so he followed it in and then captured a picture of an orb.

Voices and footsteps were heard throughout the house during both investigations. Doors opened and closed on their own, and unexplained flower-like odors were detected. Apparitions were spotted by several investigators. There were several unexplained cold spots, accompanied by positive EMF readings, and both investigations took place on warm evenings.

It definitely seems like there is substance to the ghostly experiences of those in the Winzinger family. The professional investigators produced results that would back up most of what had been seen or felt. While the ghosts cannot be identified for sure, spirit activity is there, and it could be from many sources. The house is pre–Civil War, so the Blue Ghost who looks like a soldier from that era could be a friend or family member of the Barclay Haines family. The fact that so much of the house has been brought in from so many other historic buildings that no longer exist could explain some spirits, which might have followed these artifacts;

they have nowhere else to go. JoAnn feels for many of these old buildings that have been destroyed; the spirits might be following a friendly and empathetic companion.

The spirit activity seems to surround the grounds and the immediate area of the Barclay Haines Homestead, as well. Robin now lives almost directly across the street from her parents, in a historic house that was once the "Hainesport House." Robin said in the Hainesport House's heyday, there was lodging upstairs and a restaurant downstairs. A foundry stood nearby, along the creek. Many would come from the foundry to the Hainesport House for food and shelter. They could purchase a hot meal for a dollar and get a room upstairs.

There have been many automobile accidents along that stretch of Marne Highway near the Barclay Haines Homestead and the old Hainesport House. Robin and Heidi remember as kids their mother would cover the injured with Mexican serapes to keep them warm. They also remember hearing many of those involved in accidents report seeing people cross the road; they would swear they saw something they swerved to avoid, but there was never anything or anyone there.

Could motorists have seen the spirits of those who burned the old, long toll bridge to detain the British troops? Or those who long ago crossed the highway to go to the Hainesport House for a hot meal? Or the children who drowned in the creek by the Homestead? Could it be spirit energy remaining in the planks of the wharf or the old Barclay steamer at rest in the cove?

Orbs and mists were reported outside the Homestead by SJGR during its investigations, and the grounds surrounding the Homestead seemed just as active as the rooms and staircases inside. Surrounded by water, it is not surprising that the area maintains the energy of long-ago spirits and activity. The energy at this site from the many lives that thrived and ended here, contained by the energy of the Rancocas waters, all favor spirit possibilities.

From the Patriots who perished dismantling the old toll bridge to vibrant and enterprising Barclay Haines and his family to the energy of artifacts from old buildings all over the world that JoAnn Winzinger has been bringing to this property, the possibilities for spirit existence are endless. But unless an apparition can be recognized, it remains nameless, and one can only wonder about its identity. A Leni-Lenape family from old Sandhickney? A colonial Patriot who perished in fire destroying old long bridge? Young Edda Haines, who died an early death? It could even be commuters from a London train station or vacationers from a hotel in Atlantic City demolished by Winzinger Incorporated.

We might never know who the Blue Ghost is, who sings in the piano room or who crosses the creek and the highway, but many can attest, and paranormal professionals have proven, that there are definitely spirits that are calling the Haines Homestead home.

4
NO LYIN' — THERE ARE GHOSTS AT THE LYCEUM

Anyone who thinks this world is without magic, hasn't been to a library.
—*Amy F. Dominy, American author and playwright*

At 307 High Street in Mount Holly stands the beautiful Burlington County Lyceum of History and Natural Sciences. In 1957, when Mount Holly purchased the building for its library, it became known as the Mount Holly Library, but in 2013, Burlington County took over operation and ownership of the building and officially bestowed on it the full Burlington County Lyceum designation.

While this lovely building has had several lives, it is the lives that were lived here prior to its being a library or a lyceum that are the most interesting to those who have experienced spirit activity in the building. Those lives are the ones that led Maureen Carroll, a professional paranormal researcher with SJGR to conclude, "There does appear to be layers of spirits here."

James Langstaff built this beautiful Georgian estate in 1829 from materials brought in from Pennsylvania and North Carolina that were delivered to his own personal landing on Washington Street. Back then, the Rancocas was deep, and steamships came in daily, making deliveries and transporting passengers to Philadelphia and ports beyond. He named his new home "Langleland," a Welsh term meaning "a foot of high ground."[5] Two and a half acres of land surrounded Langleland, a beautiful landscape of boxwoods and an orchard of trees, grapevines and luscious flowerbeds in the rear of the property.

Langleland was the estate of James Langstaff long before it was home to the Burlington County Lyceum of History and Natural Sciences. *Photo by Judy Gauntt.*

But times were not always joyful there. Langstaff's beloved granddaughter, Cornelia, was killed in the mansion when she was eleven years old. She was visiting with her parents when she fell over the railing of the winding central staircase, plummeting to her death three floors below. It seems the railing has never been repaired. So if you visit the lyceum, look up at the staircase, and you will see where Cornelia fell to her death.

The building has been investigated twice by South Jersey Ghost Research, once in January 2005 and more recently in August 2013. While for both times, proof of spirit activity has been documented, you might not need to be a professional ghost hunter to feel a spirit or two in this building. Several people have seen Cornelia peek playfully around the corner when children's groups are in progress. She has even appeared when library or Main Street Mount Holly meetings are in session there. Alicia McShulkis, who has served as board president of the library association, and as a Main Street Mount Holly staffer, saw Cornelia appear during one such meeting. Alicia put her index finger up to her lips to urge Cornelia to be quiet, and the little girl vanished. Alicia is "sensitive" to spirit activity, a term bestowed on those who can see or are otherwise in tune with spirits. She has had this gift her whole

The beautiful winding staircase in the center hallway of Langstaff's estate witnessed the death of his granddaughter, Cornelia. *Photo by Judy Gauntt.*

life. She has likewise seen spirit activity at the Burlington County Prison Museum; at Rock, Paper, Scissors in Mount Holly's Mill Race Village; and on many occasions in the lyceum.

Another time Cornelia appeared was on March 12, 2008. Many Mount Holly neighbors had eagerly gathered at the lyceum that evening to watch the airing of *Ghost Hunters*, which was featuring a paranormal investigation of Mount Holly's very haunted Burlington County Prison Museum, located right down High Street from the lyceum. The investigation was done by The Atlantic Paranormal Society (TAPS), one of America's best-known paranormal research groups, which hosted this series on the SyFy channel. After the show ended and people were leaving, Alicia McShulkis; her daughter, Karine; and some of the others from the library were putting things away. Karine suddenly became visibly shaken as she saw Cornelia, cast in a greenish hue, standing on the second-floor landing with her head resting on her crossed hands, not far from the place of her death.

Was Corneila there to see what the gathering was about, to see if any children had come by to play? Maybe the presence of the townspeople interested in finding out about ghosts in Mount Holly encouraged her to make an appearance, as spirits often manifest when there are people about who are open to meeting them. Since she seems to have a curious but friendly nature, she might have been hanging around to check out the fellow ghosts from the building down the street, although I'm sure her parents would not approve of her hanging out with prisoners and the like—and probably neither would Robert, although Cornelia's well-being is not quite so important to him as are the boxwoods surrounding the lyceum.

Robert is the ghost of a former groundskeeper at the mansion. Robert mostly stays outside. He stands there and watches what's going on, and he seems to be very protective about the garden and the boxwoods. He has been seen in the back of the library and outside around the boxwoods by Alicia and others. The Community Room, which is in the back on the first floor, is a modern addition to the building. In the Langstaff days, an outdoor pergola stood there, and no doubt, Robert tended to the greenery there. He probably does not realize he is inside when he is seen in this back room.

Samuel Haines, Langstaff's brother-in-law, lived at the Langstaff mansion in the 1860s, according to census reports researched by Alicia McShulkis. At a fundraiser for the library in October 2011, tarot card readers were hired to give readings to attendees. The card readers also did some Ouija board consultations, and they reported that through the Ouija board a man named Samuel was talking to them. He said that he was related to the owner of the

This back room of the lyceum is a newer addition and stands where Robert's garden once flourished. *Photo by Judy Gauntt.*

home. Well, that would be Sam Haines, brother of Harriet Haines, who married James Langstaff; he is still there! When you get to live off in-laws in a beautiful mansion, why leave?

Other residents during the Langstaff era included a coachman and his family and a housekeeper and her daughter. Dr. Daniel Reamer owned the property from about 1953 until 1957. Dr. Reamer became the county coroner, a job that I'm sure caused him to often bring his work home with him. And maybe some of the spirits followed him here, which could explain the "layers of spirit activity" investigator Maureen Carroll and her fellow ghost hunters encountered on the last South Jersey Ghost Research investigation at the lyceum.

The investigation began shortly after 9:00 p.m. on August 2, 2013. SJGR director Dave Juliano split his group into four teams, each taking a different area in the lyceum, from the basement to the attic, or third floor. As the first team to investigate the attic trudged up the stairs, investigator Wende Sutton reported that the energy markedly changed as she went from the second floor to the attic, where the temperature hit ninety-one degrees. Upon reaching the attic, the investigators reported hearing several strange sounds, including a tuba and beeping sounds. They recorded a male EVP that said, "Sexy" and a woman that said, "What do you ask me?" Two of them also experienced a disembodied voice sighing. One of the investigators, Taryn Kerper, reported that someone poked her on the butt, and none of the other investigators was near her at the time. They witnessed the planchette of a Ouija board that was in the attic room for Halloween events move around by itself.

Later, when Maureen Carroll's group was on the third floor, Mandy Little felt the presence of a young girl wearing a white nightgown and got the impression of the name "Amelia." Could that have been Cornelia? Mandy knew nothing previously about Cornelia, and that is pretty close to be just coincidence.

Later on, a male spirit tried to channel through Mandy, as the light around her would get brighter, then dim and then get brighter again. When Mandy felt something against her back, Maureen took her outside to "ground." As soon as Mandy touched the tree in front of the lyceum, the energy field around her seemed to drop, and she felt better. But when Maureen and Mandy's group later investigated the second floor, they saw who they felt to be that same male presence sitting in a chair, and he seemed very displeased that Maureen had taken Mandy away.

Also, on the second floor, several investigators sensed a female presence looking for a child. One investigator, Rose, asked her if she was afraid of them and picked up two voices on their recorder. The first was a male voice that seemed distant and said, "No," but then a closer voice answered, "Yes." They then picked up a recording of a little girl's voice singing.

The lyceum has a plaque in one of the rooms listing the names of World War I soldiers from the area. Coincidently (or not), on the first floor, investigators Marti Haines and Kathy Smith encountered a couple soldiers. One was older and heavily decorated. The other was a World War I doughboy. He seemed very distressed and was looking for his mother. He indicated that he did not return home from the war or possibly did not return home in time. Marti felt pain in her chest, as if from a gunshot, while Kathy felt pain in her chest and lungs, which could have been from a physical wound or deep, emotional sorrow. The presence appeared to be deeply grieving, and Marti strongly empathized with the spirit. She asked Kathy to be sure nobody else entered the room, as she was going to do a blessing for the young soldier.

Often during investigations, spirit energy and emotions are experienced by the investigators, and this is what was happening this evening with several of them. Feelings of sorrow, nausea, headaches and other sensations often overcome investigators and mediums, as the spirits can transfer energy and emotions as a way of manifesting. It is a strong indication of ghostly presence.

Researchers even found activity in the basement of the lyceum that night. Investigators encountered a little boy in a white shirt and suspenders and an older man, both hired to work in an orchard. The Langstaffs had a large orchard behind their residence. Could the man have been Robert? Several investigators also reported feeling something moving around their ankles while in the basement and several unexplained shadows were reported, one moving over the room and then another, darting out of the room. Investigator Mike Little saw an apparition of a female spirit, a woman that Mandy had felt impressions of in the kitchen on the first floor. Then, Mandy felt someone touch her face, and at that moment, a voice was recorded saying, "You understand."

All of the investigators, in each of the four groups, reported the change in energy as they climbed the stairs. Juliano is the only one of those participating who was present for the investigation in 2005, and most of the investigators knew nothing about the history of the building or Cornelia being killed there. Juliano stated that there was a woman at the top of the stairs, leaning on the banister. Both he and Marti felt that she was grieving or possibly contemplating suicide. "This could be residual energy, I'm not sure, but it is very strong. We all felt it," he recalled.

But Juliano questions the accidental nature of the death that occurred. He is not sure if the female is experiencing guilt or grief. "Something isn't right about falling down the stairs. At least five people that night picked up on this. Somebody was doing something she should not have been."

Dave lay on the floor in the staircase area for quite a while that night, taking pictures. "It was just so compelling," he said. But none of the pictures came out. Kathy Smith reported that her recorder had fresh batteries and was on the whole time, but when she played it back later, it was blank—classic ghostly pranks. Do I hear Cornelia laughing?

5

FROM PEMBERTON WITH LOVE

THE HAUNTING OF WELLSMERE

*Perhaps they are not stars in the sky, but rather openings where our loved ones
shine down and let us know they are happy.*
—*Charlie Brown (Charles Schultz)*

In the 1770s, New Mills, about seven miles east of Mount Holly and bordering
the pinelands, was a bustling little Burlington County village, inhabited by
about one hundred households and surrounded by many prosperous farms.
Besides the sawmill and gristmill, establishments for which the little hamlet
earned its name, New Mills had several other businesses, including a cobbler
shop, a tavern and a company store. Burlington County's first company town
was bookended with a Baptist church at one end and a Methodist church at
the other, making it a religious epicenter for those two congregations.

Over the subsequent decades, New Mills became prosperous and grew. In
1822, a stagecoach line started taking passengers in the area to Philadelphia,
and New Mills became a stop along that line. In 1825, another stage line
came though New Mills in the summer, stopping to pick up passengers for
trips through the New Jersey pinelands to the seashore.

On December 15, 1826, New Mills became incorporated as Pemberton
Borough. Holding its first election the following May, the town elected
Samuel W. Budd as its first mayor. The very first ordinance passed by the
Honorable Mr. Budd and his council was to outlaw swine from running
freely in the streets.

In 1829, the town council passed ordinances officially naming those swine-
free streets. Main Street became Hanover Street. Budd Street might have been

named in tribute to the first mayor, and other streets were named for families who had a stake in the development of the borough, including Reynolds, Lacey and Hough. Some were named for the daughters of early landowners and businessmen, like Elizabeth Street and Jane Street. In 1837, the railroad came through Pemberton, running from Philadelphia to the seashore, increasing trade and travel along the way, as well as the prosperity of Pemberton.

On January 20, 1844, Davis Coward Wells was born in nearby Vincentown. He married Mary Adelaide Reid in 1873. Listed as a stockholder of the Burlington County Agricultural Society, he was also owner of the Pemberton Drug Store and a shoe factory. He was a man of prominence in society and very popular socially as well, even fielding first base on the Pemberton baseball team.

In 1882, Davis Wells built his home on Elizabeth Street on the block that spans Hough to Egbert Street, stretching down the south side to the edge of the Rancocas Creek. Wellsmere, as he named his homestead, was a mansion of novel, Queen Anne–Victorian design, with no detail neglected.

He encased the front of his mansion with a beautiful wraparound porch and a porte-cochere on the west side of the veranda to shelter those arriving by horse and carriage. A majestic widow's tower crowned the grand entrance, which had large, carved double doors flanked by stained-glass windows and opened to a wide, ornate staircase. The magnificent staircase beckons you to the second floor, making it hard to decide whether to climb or to languish in the splendid parlor with ceiling-to-floor bay windows. Towering twelve-foot ceilings were trimmed with plaster moldings and graced with ornate medallions that framed gas-powered chandeliers. Pocket doors separated the parlor from the secondary rooms on the first floor, and all the walls were lavishly papered.

Davis built service quarters for his staff, on the Hough Street side of the property. The former servants' housing still stands as a private residence today. Quite self-sufficient, Davis even erected a windmill on the property and pumped water into his home from the creek. He also built an icehouse on the Egbert Street side of the property and had ice dragged from the creek in the winter and stored it in this icehouse, which later residents of the home would use as a garage. He also smoked his own meat and hung the carcasses on hooks in a room on the third floor. Until the most recent owners, Dave and Gina Barry, remodeled the upper floors, the sharp hooks and the blood stains of the animals were still on the walls of that room.

In addition to the ornate details, Davis and Mary Wells filled their mansion with seven children. One son, Harold, would become very well educated

Davis Wells's remarkable Victorian estate, built in 1892, is a home some have trouble leaving. *Photo by Chas Bastien.*

and a successful lawyer, later appointed to a Burlington County judgeship. In years to come, this grand mansion would host the high-society weddings of several of their children. Sadly, Wellsmere would also provide the setting for the funeral of their thirteen-month-old daughter, Helen, on February 20, 1885, at 11:00 a.m.

In May 1894, Davis C. Wells was elected chief burgess of the town council. Later that month, there was a devastating fire in Pemberton that destroyed much of the midtown, including seven homes, the Methodist church, two stores, three barns and a row of horse sheds. The blaze threatened to wipe out the entire town, summoning responders from as far away as Camden. According to Judy Olsen, author of *Pemberton, An Historic Look at a Village on the Rancocas*, "a Philadelphia newspaper photographer took a photograph during the immediate aftermath of the fire while the buildings were still smoldering and one of his photos showed a ghostly image of a young boy. There wasn't a building for him to haunt as most of the block was rubble. I never heard that anyone felt the boy appeared after the fire."[6] But he could have been leaving a building that he was haunting before the fire. A ghost needs energy to manifest, and the heat from the fire could have provided him that.

After the fire, Wells became a charter stockholder of the Pemberton Water Works, formed to prevent future fire disasters. Despite his fire prevention efforts, Davis C. Wells couldn't protect his beloved Wellsmere from suffering a fire in 1912. On May 19 of that year, the twelve-year-old daughter of Harry Brown, one of Davis's staff, went to search for something in a clothes closet on the third floor, lighting her way with an oil lamp. The flame from the lamp ignited her clothing. She screamed, and her breath further fueled the flames. When members of the household responding to her aid got there, she was "a mass of flames," as reported in the *New Jersey Mirror*. She was rushed to Burlington County Hospital, but she died the next day.

Davis C. Wells died three years later himself, on January 12, 1915, and was buried four days after that in Odd Fellows Cemetery in Pemberton Township. His wife, Mary, hosted their daughter Mary Marguerite's wedding at Wellsmere in September 1919, but it was a quiet affair with only relatives in attendance, as Mrs. Wells herself was ill and near the end of her life.

Wellsmere has had many owners and has seen many changes since the Wells family left in the early twentieth century. As, unfortunately, often happens to beautiful old mansions, sometime in the mid-1900s it was divided into two residences, 27 and 29 Elizabeth Street, and 27, the western side residence, was further split into two apartments. While still a magnificent residence, there were times that parts of the home went neglected, yet there were also post-Wells owners and renters who took care of it, refurbished it and relished in its grandeur.

Two of the most recent owners of Wellsmere have experienced unusual stirrings in this house that could be related to paranormal activities. Many attribute these stirrings to Harry Brown's daughter, who perished in the May 1912 fire on the third floor.

In 1985, about a year after Chas Bastien purchased 29 Elizabeth, the eastern half of the house, his neighbor renting 27 came to him, visibly shaken, and said, "Man, I just dozed off on the couch upstairs, and when I woke up, this little girl was staring at me. She just stood there and kept staring at me. Then, like, poof! She disappeared. She didn't walk away or anything; she was just gone!" This tenant knew nothing about Wellsmere history or the little girl who died there.

The little girl has appeared to others in Wellsmere, as well. In 1990, Bill, a tenant renting the second-floor apartment of 27, saw a little girl in a lace dress at the top of the steps leading to the third floor. She just stood there and looked down at him.

One day in 1993, when Chas Bastien was leaving the house, a brass chalice fell off a table in the corner of his dining room. Running late, he left it there.

When he returned home that evening, it was back on the table. Except for Ginger, he was living alone in Wellsmere at the time.

Ginger was Bastien's red Doberman, fearless of most people, and she would not go in the room on the third floor, where Wells hung his smoked meat. Ginger would stand near the door and, no matter how much her master coaxed her, would not cross the threshold.

When I married Chas Bastien in 1995, I moved into Wellsmere and, at the time, knew nothing of these hauntings. But in January of that year, my sister, Barbara Cranmer, was our guest at Wellsmere, staying at 29 Elizabeth. When she came down for breakfast in the morning, she asked who the little girl was who appeared in the hallway outside her second-floor bedroom door. Barbara had witnessed an apparition of a little girl, all white, looking into the bedroom, probably wondering who the stranger was in that room. This was the first time Barbara, who lives nowhere near Pemberton, had ever stayed at Wellsmere, and she knew nothing of the history of the house or the death of the little girl. "She didn't scare me, she seemed sweet and peaceful and very curious."

In 2004, Chas Bastien and I sold 29 Elizabeth Street, our share of Wellsmere, to Dave and Gina Barry, formerly of Philadelphia. At that time, 27 belonged to somebody else, and several years later, it went into foreclosure and was left abandoned in total shambles and disrepair. What a fate for a home of such grand stature and admiration. However, eventually, the Barrys bought 27, now owning Wellsmere in its grand entirety, and they are making major renovations to the estate, enabling it to regain the dignity it deserves.

One day in 2011, soon after side 27 was gutted to begin the renovations, Dave and Gina were on the second floor, observing the work that had been done thus far. They heard heavy footsteps on the second floor. They were sure they were alone in the house, but they kept calling, "Hello? Hello?" because it sounded so loud and near. They got no response.

"We were standing at the rear staircase, which we have since removed," Gina recalled. "The footsteps were coming from the front. It was very loud." But nobody else was there—except maybe Davis and Mary Wells, inspecting the work being done on their beloved mansion.

Frequently, Gina feels she is not alone and senses there is something going on. During construction, there were often the sounds of doors slamming, even where there were no longer doors.

Gina frequently hears the sound of a woman walking in high heels across the upper floors, usually from the front of the house. She also often gets the smell of perfume, just a breeze wafting by. Could it be Mrs. Wells? Or could the little Brown girl be dressing up in her mother's clothes, as little girls often do? Could she also be wearing Mrs. Wells's perfume?

At this time, nobody is living in 27, but it seems like somebody does like the brand-new kitchen. Gina often smells food cooking when nobody is cooking on either side of the house. One day in 2012, Gina placed a copy of the new Burlington County phone book on the kitchen island they had just installed in 27. When she went back, it was on the third step going up to the third floor. Maybe the ghostly cook doesn't like the island cluttered.

Gina claims she is not afraid of her company in Wellsmere and gets the feeling the spirits are content and pleased with the fact that they are restoring the home. "It actually seems to have settled down as we are completing renovations. There was a lot more activity earlier during construction."

It is said that houses have souls. I have lived in Wellsmere myself, and I know this grand mansion has a grand soul. The energy is overwhelmingly good there, and decorating and entertaining in this fine home can give one such pleasure. I am sure that Davis Wells and his family loved it even more than I did and that they have found it hard to leave, as I did. I am sure the little girl in the lace dress loved the adventure of its many rooms and staircases, the closets, the widow's tower and other places to hide and play. If the spirits of the Wells family remain, I am sure they had their times of concern when their grand home fell into disrepair and stuck around to oversee and protect it. But they must be happy again with the love and care the entire structure is now receiving. The soul of Wellsmere must feel as soothed with the thoughtful restorations as the spirits that remain there.

6

THE LIBRARY COMPANY OF BURLINGTON

A PLACE WITH SPIRITED READING

Libraries are the heart of every community, keeping our minds and spirits alive.
—*Gail Lukasik, American author*

While a library can have an influence on a person's life, the influence usually comes from the books that one borrows or maybe the programs one attends. The resources available at the library might help mold your career or enrich your hobbies. But for Sharon Vincz, director of the Library Company of Burlington, working at the library led her to become a ghost hunter.

Chartered by King George II in 1757, the Library Company of Burlington is the oldest library in continuous operation in New Jersey, and the seventh oldest in the nation. In 1758, it was the first library in the United States to publish a library catalogue, listing the over seven hundred books donated by its charter members. The oldest book in the library's collection was written in 1551, and it counts among its artifacts several volumes written by William Penn.

Before the beautiful West Union Street brownstone was constructed, the Library Company led a nomadic life, starting out in a room at the home of Thomas Rodman, one of its two founding members. Its collections then moved among several other members' homes in the early years before the Library Company found its first permanent structure on Library Street in 1789, where it laid down stakes for seventy-five years. Then, James Sterling, who had been the director for decades, presented the library with a posthumous gift, but it was tied to a challenge. He bequeathed the library

$5,000 to find or build a new structure, if it could accomplish this within two years of his death. Many prominent Burlingtonians rallied around the cause, including Mrs. Julia Grant, wife of General Ulysses S. Grant, who lived nearby on Wood Street. Because of the commitment and diligence of the people of Burlington, the library found and purchased the land, and the building was constructed. In 1864, within the allotted time frame, the Library Company opened its doors on 23 West Union Street. It has been there continuously, and in 1957, ground was broken for a new addition in the back to house the Children's Room.

When you enter this lovely nineteenth-century building, you will find the winding staircase on the right is roped off. Sharon said it is so people don't just wander up there, but Sandy Santucci, a former staffer who worked there for thirty-six years, doesn't care if the ropes are there or not; she has no intention of going up there, anyway. Why? One day, shortly after she had reported for work and was putting books in the back office, she heard a loud crash on the third floor near the top of the staircase. She ran up the steps, expecting to find something fallen or broken; she searched and found nothing. Nothing fallen, nothing broken and nobody up there. Nobody could have snuck past her on that narrow, winding staircase. There was no explanation, but there was no mistake she heard it. She just chalked it up to another one of the many unexplained happenings at the library, like the sound of the soldiers often heard marching in the basement.

Sharon's experiences at the library are also rich with spirit encounters, and they have really piqued her interest in the paranormal. If you have an open mind, ghosts often feel more comfortable making themselves known to you, and such is the case with Sharon. While still remaining skeptical, she is open to the possibility of sharing her space with energies that come from the other side. Her experiences here at the Library Company have added to her conviction that some of those who have physically left might still spiritually remain, and while her "day job" might be director of the Library Company of Burlington, she is also a trained and certified professional ghost hunter with South Jersey Ghost Research (SJGR).

Let's climb that winding staircase by the front door and venture up to the third floor of the Library Company building. Up here, the old floorboards croak and groan. While that could just be due to the age of the building, some things do go unexplained up here, and many people, especially women, often feel uncomfortable. Sharon reports that "many women get the feeling that they are being 'pushed out,'" while some mediums have sensed there are men in the meeting room.

This nineteenth-century library was the result of the commitment of many Burlingtonians, including the wife of General Ulysses S. Grant.

These feelings are well founded. In the early years of the Burlington Library Company's residence on West Union Street, it was up here on the third floor that the Free and Accepted Masons held their regular meetings. While the library has no documentation of the times or dates of the meetings of this esoteric society, Sharon stated that the library believes the room was originally built for the Masons to use.

"We can tell from the way the room was designed," said Sharon. "The peep holes, the area for the guard to stand, the back room for a holding room prior to entry, two entrance doors into the room, the raised floor forming a stage-like area, the secret auger hole where the floor opened up to store their ritual books and materials" all lead library historians to believe that this room was specifically designed for the Masons to hold their restricted and closely guarded meetings.

The first time that South Jersey Ghost Research (SJGR) conducted a paranormal investigation here in June 2007, they felt heavy spirit energy, especially in the Gallery, in the third-floor area where the Masons met, and also in the Resource Room, which is just nearby. They have since investigated the Library Company building on several occasions and occasionally host presentations there. During one of the public ghost hunting presentations, Russell Horrocks and his wife, Gail, were present. They live across the Delaware River in Bucks County but became supporters of the Library Company because Gail was a teacher at the Wilbur Watts Intermediate School in Burlington City. Russell has also served as the worshipful master of a Masonic Lodge in Jenkintown, Pennsylvania. Upon going up to the third floor, Russell verified that this room was definitely built to be used by the Masons. He told SJGR that there is certain furniture in the room that is significant; for instance, the alter in the room is typical of one that would be in a Masonic Hall and is where the Bible would be placed. Other shelving and built-ins were also typical, including the stage-type raised floor under the large windows on the back side of the room. He, therefore, feels the room must have been specifically designed to hold Masonic meetings.

Worshipful Master Horrocks approached the front of the room and suddenly felt the temperature change. "That's when I knew something was going on," he remembered. "I announced who I was and welcomed them to communicate with me. Then I walked to the front and sat quietly, waiting." Then the EMF meters went off.

He performed certain knocks that are known to Masons and asked for signs. "The energy in the room suddenly changed, and all the investigators felt it," remembered SJGR director Dave Juliano, who led the investigation that night. The female investigators reported feeling particularly unwelcome.

Among the equipment SJGR brought with them on that investigation was an Ovilus, an electronic speech-synthesis device that produces real words from changes in environmental readings, including electromagnetic waves. Paranormal researchers theorize that spirits may be able to alter environmental factors such as electromagnetic frequencies and temperature. The Ovilus picks up on these changes in energy and is able to produce words, helping the investigator to communicate with ghosts.

"I started asking them questions that only a Mason would know the answers to, and the answers came through on the Ovilus. One thing I remember distinctly is that when I asked for a sign of something that is

The Masonic Altar was a centerpiece in their meetings held here in the early days of the library.

significant to Masons, the spirits said '7.' I could not think of any way that the number 7 was significant to the Masons. Then, I started counting the letters of the alphabet, and 'G' is the seventh letter. They had me going on that; that one took a while," laughed Horrocks. If you have seen the Masonic symbol, you know it prominently displays a capital *G*.

A male voice from the past came through strongly that night on the Ovilus, Juliano remembered. The spirit introduced himself as a World War II glider pilot. He gave them directions to a memorial in Burlington, in front of the American Legion, which is dedicated to those in the community who made the supreme sacrifice in World War II. "We were not at all aware of that monument or its location, until this ghost told us about it," stated Juliano. But it is there, in front of the American Legion, along the banks of the Delaware River.

The worshipful master and the SJGR investigators then went downstairs to continue their work, searching through the stacks for evidence of the paranormal. They had EMF readers with them, which they noticed were going off in certain places, but not others. So the next time the EMF reader went off, an investigator pulled the closest book off the shelf. Horrocks looked at the book and said it was written by a fellow Mason. The next time the EMF meter went off, they again pulled the closest book, and sure enough, it was another booked penned by a Mason. They started waving the EMF reader in front of books. Every time it went off, the book by the meter was either written by a Mason or was written about a Mason. No other books had the energy to set the EMF reader off. And once the meter identified the book as being about or by a Mason, it did not go off again by that book, either. It seems that when the worshipful master invited his brethren to speak to him, they were happy to oblige.

Now, there is another book written by a Mason that has a special place at the Library Company. Go back upstairs to the Masonic meeting room, and you'll find it there in a glass book case. It's a small, leather-bound book simply titled *Baukalendar*. The title, the date 1882 and the emblem of the Free and Accepted Masons, the square and compass with the *G*, are all that is on the worn, leather book cover. It is a journal that belonged to a German gentleman with the surname of Doherty. Herr Doherty dutifully chronicled his days in it, recording many details, including the weather and other happenings.

One of Sharon's fellow SJGR investigators, Mike Zahn, came into possession of this book after one of his clients found it. Whenever the client opened the book and attempted to read it to her husband, strange things would happen in her house; shadows would appear, and she became frightened. She was positive the eerie happenings were coming from the book and felt she could not keep the book in her home any longer, so she gave it to Zahn. The first thing Mike did was to put the book in a bag of sea salt for a month to settle the book's very strong energy; it is believed that negative energy can't live in the same place as salt, and this practice is often used when spirits are very strong, especially if they are thought to be negative or very resistant. At the end of the cleansing period, he donated the book to the Library Company of Burlington on behalf of SJGR, handing it to Sharon in the plastic bag. Sharon was wary at first, but they placed it in

What secrets are contained in the diary of a deceased German gentleman?

the book case, on the third floor, where the Masons met. Herr Doherty was told that the Masons are here and he is among friends; they told him he is welcome to stay here, as long as everyone is happy.

"Mason energy is different," Sharon said. "They are at a distance, kind of standoffish, but they are watching you. You feel it. And women and men often feel it differently. Women who come up here often get the feeling they are being pushed out. It's like you can feel the presence of the male guard in the doorway, and he doesn't want you in here." SJGR investigator and medium Marti Haines also feels like she is not welcomed by the male guard at the door to the Masons' meeting room, and she gets a bad feeling if she touches Doherty's book.

And Brother Doherty's book, resting in the case in the Mason's meeting area, has an energy of its own. Sharon feels his energy whenever she comes up here. He knows she is here, and he makes his presence known to her. And if somebody messes with the book, Sharon always knows, even if she is not in the room; she feels he is letting her know. While the general energy from the past Masons is constantly present, but distanced, Doherty's energy "is right there," said Sharon. "It's on you."

In 2012, SJGR hosted an investigation joined by the NEPA Ghost Detectives, a paranormal investigation group based in Pennsylvania. It was the Ghost Detectives' first visit to the Library Company, and they knew nothing about the *Baukalendar* or where in the library it was located. Sharon wrote down the name of the book on a piece of paper, folded it up and placed it in her office, under her mouse pad, without showing anyone. Using dowsing rods, Katy, one of the Ghost Detectives' crew, asked the spirits to lead her to the book that Sharon had secretly identified. The rods led her through the stacks, past all the possibilities of books, and then up the stairs. Within ten minutes, the dowsing rods went off at the book case and pointed at the *Baukalendar*.

"It seems to say this? Could that be right?" Katy seemed surprised that it was this little journal she was led to and not one of the more impressive volumes in the library. Sharon nodded her head "yes" and revealed the paper where she had simply written *Baukalendar*. Then, SJGR investigators brought their Ovilus over to the bookcase; it produced a male voice, counting backward in German.

From November 2007 through February 2008, the Library Company hosted a fascinating exhibit of vintage wedding gowns in the old Masonic meeting room. The beautiful Victorian display was one of the highlights of the Burlington City Holiday House Tour. During these several months while the collection was in the room, the lights would constantly turn on by themselves, and that had nothing to do with holiday decorating. An insomniac neighbor of the library called Sharon on many occasions and told her that even in the middle of the night, when nobody was there, the lights were going on and off. So, doing her due diligence as the library's director, Sharon contacted a local certified electrician to have the electric system checked out. The electrician said he would be there in two weeks, but when Sharon stressed that it was for a historic building, he came right over. He carefully went throughout the building, checking the complete electric system, and finding nothing wrong, he slapped it with a clean bill of health. "So, we had no explanation for the phenomenon," Sharon stated, but she knew the gowns had to come out of the library. When the display came down and the gowns were gone, there were no more problems with errant electricity.

No "normal" explanation for the electrical phenomenon, maybe, but as Sharon and other experienced paranormal investigators know, spirits often harness the energy in an electrical system to manifest. The more mischievous ghosts also love to play pranks on people or, if they are perturbed about something, will do anything to get your attention and let you know about it. Fooling around with the lights and using the energy from electricity is very common, according to paranormal research. Could the old Masons have been taunting, or even flirting with, the Victorian ladies taking up residence on their "turf"? Or maybe they were trying to let Sharon know she had stepped over the line by putting the ladies in their meeting room.

While Herr Doherty and his Masonic brothers keep things interesting on the third floor, the basement of this historic library is where the spirit activity seems to be the strongest. There are old newspapers stored in the back of the basement that have been with the Library Company since they were in their former building. Some of these papers are from as far back as 1833; imagine the energy that must be stored in them! Also felt in the basement is the spirit of a soldier whom many have heard marching; some mediums have even seen him but can't identify the period of his garb. But the building opened during the Civil War period, and up on the third floor is a bust of General Edward Burd Grubb. He was a Union commander in the American Civil War, and he was born in Burlington. Maybe General Grubb has come home.

There is also in the basement an eleven-year-old girl, whose EVPs show up during paranormal investigations. Marti Haines has been able to communicate with her, and some investigators have encountered another little girl playing with her. There's also an older guy wearing overalls; he hangs out on the back steps. All these basement spirits have been revealed to investigators and mediums on paranormal investigations.

While investigating the basement with the NEPA Ghost Detectives in 2012, Sharon and the SJGR crew heard a child's giggle, and one of the crew of detectives felt someone of short stature tap his elbow. He placed a flashlight on the shelf and said, "If that was you, sweetheart, turn on this flashlight for us." At first, nothing happened, but after a few minutes, the flashlight came on all by itself.

Done fighting Confederates, has General Grubb come home to the library that was built while he fought in the Civil War?

And then there is Charlie. He's here most of the time, and everyone seems to know him. Several investigators and mediums, independently and on separate occasions, have picked up on him and identified him as a spirit named "Charlie." There once was a man named Charlie who was a caretaker at the library, and Sharon believes it is his spirit watching over things in the basement. SJGR case notes from its June 29, 2007 investigation concur, identifying Charlie's spirit as "a male spirit in the unfinished portion of the basement; a protective presence in the library, but one who resents any intrusion into 'his' space."[7]

Sharon remembered the early days of her relationship with Charlie. "We used to have arguments. When I started here, this room was a mess. The insurance company was coming to do a walk-through, and I was told I had to clean it up. So I went down to get started one day. Almost as soon as I opened the door, I was overcome with a full-blown cat allergy attack! I had to go back upstairs, and then I went home and got allergy pills. I tried again the next day, and it happened again. I finally went back and tried to work things out with Charlie. 'Stop putting that cat in my face!' I told him." She began to reason with Charlie, and after a few weeks, they came to an understanding and now respect each other. "I appreciate him so much!" said Sharon. But when SJGR did an investigation in the basement, one of the mediums saw a cat run though it.

After one SJGR investigation, Marti Haines told Sharon that Charlie wanted to know how Edgar was doing. "Edgar?" Sharon wracked her brain and couldn't figure out who Edgar was. She finally realized he meant Tom Edgar, the owner of the Café Gallery, a restaurant that had been a landmark in Burlington for years and still was at that time. Tom lived next door and was a friend of the Library Company. Charlie must have taken a liking to him.

Once, Sharon researched a document for the wife of one of the Library Company's trustees. To show their appreciation, they gave Sharon a bottle of fifty-year-old Scotch. She left it in her office, on the first floor, for a while and then took it home, unopened. When SJGR was performing a subsequent investigation, Sharon was up on the second floor when one of the investigators checking out the basement came and got her to ask her to come down to the basement. Charlie was present and demanded to know what happened to the Scotch! "He must have gone into my office!" she gasped. "I never brought it down here!" Laughing, she told them to tell him that next investigation, she'd bring him Scotch.

And so she did. "Take it to Charlie," she instructed the investigators. They took it down and left it in the basement. Sharon went into the basement afterward and smelled the strong odor of a person who had been heavily drinking.

In the 2012 investigation with the NEPA Ghost Detectives, the crew had heard of Charlie's affinity for alcohol and tried to coax him into communication by offering some hooch. They placed a bottle of Scotch on the steps and one of them said, "Charlie, would you come out and have a drink with me?" Soon after that, several investigators thought they heard a voice. The investigator who made the invitation to Charlie looked at the EVP meter, and it had recorded a voice saying, "Yeah" very clearly and then a few more words after that, which they couldn't make out.

"The most recent investigation he said he wanted vodka," Sharon laughed. "So Marti brought it for him."

"Charlie keeps an eye out for us. It wouldn't be the same without him," smiles Sharon. So why shouldn't a good spirit have some good spirits once in a while?

With Sharon's position at the library, her affiliation with SJGR as a trained paranormal investigator and the heavy spirit activity in the building, she often collaborates with SJGR to host fundraising events at the library, which, of course, are centered on ghost hunting. People are so interested in ghosts that events like Spooky Shelves, Ghost Hunting 101 and Your Ghost Story are very well attended. During an SJGR Ghost Hunting 101 presentation, one of the participants noticed that one of the drawers of an old card catalogue cabinet in the back of the basement was open, so she shut it. She came back a little while later, and it had opened again, apparently on its own. There was a guy from Boston in the group, and he asked if he could take a picture of it. When he walked over, he noticed that the card sticking up identified a book, *Dancing with the Dead*, a book not available at the Library Company of Burlington. Was a spirit inviting someone in the group to dance?

SJGR also likes to do investigative training for children here as it feels that while the library is very active with spirit activity, the activity is very positive. Every child is required to be accompanied by a parent, and they are taught to be serious and respectful while ghost hunting. SJGR investigator Kim Pietrzack brought her eight-year-old son with her to one of these programs. They were in the new part of the basement, an area where they often hear noises and footsteps. Her son was playing with a flashlight, the kind that can go from white light to red or green. He clicked it on the red, and a voice on the Ovilus at that moment clearly said, "Boy…flashlight…squeeze green." And even though it was quite dark in the room, they could see the outline of figures moving about.

In 2008, there was renovation work being done in this new part of the basement, which is under the addition added in the late 1950s. "During this time, we seemed to have more unusual occurrences happening," remembered Sharon. On December 1 of that year, one of her staffers said to Sharon, "You fixed the clock!" Confused, Sharon asked her what clock she was referring to.

"The clock that hangs over the library mezzanine area; last night at about 6:30, I looked at the clock to check the time, and the hands began to spin around and around very fast. I asked Sandy to look at the clock, and we both stood there and just watched the hands spinning and spinning for some time."

"That clock is battery operated, not powered by electricity, so there was no accounting for the spinning," explained Sharon. Ghosts, as we know, often play with electricity and have often done so frequently at the library, but Sharon and her staff have no explanation for this phenomenon with that battery-operated clock. Even stranger, the next morning, the clock was set on the correct time perfectly, and nobody can explain how it set itself.

Two nights later, on December 3, the same staff member went down into the old part of the basement to check it out and turn off the lights. After she turned them out, she took out the trash and then noticed that the lights were back on again in the meeting room area, which is in the new area of the basement. She then had to return and go back down the stairs and turn the lights out again.

In the late spring of the following year, a member of the library staff went into the old part of the basement, where Charlie, the soldier, the little girl and the old guy wearing overalls have been seen by ghost hunters. She went down there just to put up some boxes and magazines. Suddenly, she heard footsteps walking right behind her. Nobody else had gone down with her, yet she suddenly knew she was not really alone. She didn't hang around long enough to find out which of the spirits was following her; she just ran out of the basement as fast as she could.

Spirit activity at the Library Company does not limit itself to the basement or the third floor. The first floor, the main floor, is also quite active. The spirits might be a little more discreet, but they still make themselves known.

Sharon knows that the ghost of Mary Martin, a librarian from 1867, hangs out on the first floor and likes to make herself known to patrons of the library. One day in March 2012, a woman was studying on the first floor, and another was nearby looking at a DVD. They both heard a voice say, "I can see you" and quickly looked up at each other. Neither had said a word, and when they started to discuss what had just happened, Mary reprimanded them with a stern *shhh*.

There is a plaque of Diane Berry, another former librarian, hanging in the main hall. Once during an SJGR event, medium Marti Haines got the strong feeling that somebody in the group knew Ms. Berry. She acknowledged her feeling to the group and said, "OK, who here knows this woman?" A big guy in the group got up and said it was his mother. Marti took him outside and spoke to him. "Diane is here," she told the man. "She asks that you not go to the cemetery anymore. She is not there. She is here, at the library." The man was shaken, but he did return. On that next visit, he donated a book to the Library Company in honor of his mother—or was it for his mother?

One of the former library directors told Sharon that she believes the ghost of Lydia Weston, a former head librarian, haunts that newer back room. She worked here from the late 1800s until she died in 1915. The library even closed for the day of her funeral. Sharon has also felt Lydia's presence, including a few times when she has dropped a book at Sharon's feet, giving Sharon the feeling she was nudging her to get back to work. Why would Lydia be in the new addition, a part that was not there during her tenure? Probably she is just curious, as spirits often are. She probably roams throughout the library, keeping an eye on things.

One morning in June 2008, Sharon was walking on the main floor from the back, newer addition into the older, front part of the building. Sandy was at her desk in the front, and Jane, another staffer, was straightening up books in the back. "When I got right where the old section and the new room join, I heard my name, 'Sharon,' right in my left ear." The voice was loud, clear and unquestionable, deep and female. She suddenly turned, expecting to bump into Jane, only to find Jane was all the way in the back of the room! Sharon went over to Sandy's desk, sat down, frazzled and whispered to her, "They know my name!"

Sharon's office is on the main floor, in the front and to the left when you come in. It's a nice office with a very historic feel to it. It seems the spirits find it quite welcoming and comfortable, as well. Sharon recalled one day in particular, April 16, 2008. She was working in her office when she suddenly got the feeling that someone was with her, and the hair on the back of her neck rose. "I know you are here," she said to the spirit, who she believes to be the ghost of William B. Allen, a former trustee. He then hit the arm of her chair sharply, twice.

"OK, you can have it for forty-five minutes. Then you have to leave; I have work to get done, too," she bargained with Allen's ghost. Sharon left

Above: Head librarian Lydia Weston (right) and assistant Hanna Severns still keep things quiet at the library. *Photo from 1915, courtesy of the Library Company of Burlington.*

Right: William B. Allen, a longtime library trustee and instrumental to the erection of the building, sometimes exercises his authority at the library today.

her office and went to work elsewhere in the library for a while. When she returned, all was calm in her office. William B. Allen was a trustee of the Library Company from 1835 to 1848 and again from 1849 to 1864, during the time when efforts to erect the current library building were underway. So during his trusteeship, the Library Company was not even on this site yet. Since the current building opened in 1864, as his term came to an end, maybe Mr. Allen feels that he missed out on the new digs and is hanging around now, enjoying its amenities and basking in the rewards of the efforts he contributed to make this historic and beautiful library a reality.

7
GHOST HUNTING AT 16 CHURCH STREET

The dead are living all around us, watching with eager anticipation how we will handle the opportunities they left in our hands when they died.
—Reverend Theodore C. Speers, chaplain,
U.S. Military Academy at West Point, 1959

In the early 1900s, the American textile industry was changing; manufacturers were inventing new, synthetic fabrics to compete with the mills in Europe. In Mount Holly, there were several mills that helped to keep area workers employed, even through the Great Depression. One such mill was the Alexander Plush Textile Mill, manufacturers of heavy-duty upholstery fabric. Their mill was located on Church Street, in the center of what is now Mount Holly's Mill Race Village. Joe Arndt was working at a mill in Philadelphia, and when he got a job at Alexander Plush in the early 1930s, he moved to Mount Holly with his young wife, Edith. They rented a duplex at 16 Church Street, adjacent to Alexander Plush.

Edith never liked going into the basement of their new home. She always felt like something was down there. Joe brushed off his wife's complaints as silly, until one day she felt someone push her and fell down the stairs. She was the only one home at the time, but when Joe came home from work, he got an earful. Edith stated she could no longer live in that house with whatever was down in the basement and swore it was some type of evil spirit. She demanded that they move. So when the adjoining house at 14 Church Street went up for sale a short while later, Joe and Edith bought it and moved next door. They lived there for the rest of their lives, which was 1984 for Edith and 1997 for Joe.

Edith and Joe had two children, who gave them four grandchildren. Their daughter, Ruth, married William Hollowell, and they had two sons, Ronald and Allan. Allan was six years old when his parents got divorced, and he and Ronnie went with his mother to live at his grandparents for the next six years. To this day, Allan does not believe that his grandparents freed themselves from ghostly activity by moving to the other side of that duplex.

One clear, summer day when Allan was about nine years old, he was sitting in his grandmother's dining room. Back then, there was no air conditioning in the house, so the screened windows and doors were open. As he sat at the table, he was amazed to watch a round, shiny, translucent object, about the size of a softball, float through the front door, down the steps to the dining room, through the door to the kitchen and out the back door, all the while remaining about three feet above the floor. To this day, Allan, now retired from a technical career, believes he witnessed an orb.

Many think of orbs as the spots you sometimes get when you take a photo, and controversy exits over whether they are truly ghosts attempting to manifest. Much of this controversy is over the atmospheric conditions, cleanliness of the lens, etc., but paranormal researchers do believe that, if questionable conditions can be ruled out, an orb can indeed be proof of spirit presence. But this translucent ball was just there and was seen by the naked eye, not a camera lens.

According to research done by Drs. Miceal Ledwith and Klauss Heinemann in the *Orb Project*, "only when orbs gather a sufficient collection of free electrons to themselves do they become visible to the camera; when that collection reaches a sufficient density they can also become visible to the naked eye."[8] Since this ball consistently hovered at about three feet from the ground, even when going down steps, if it was a spirit attempting to manifest, it was probably the ghost of a child and, therefore, was likely to have a lot of energy.

When Joe Arndt died in 1997, Allan cleaned up his grandfather's house and prepared it for sale. One of the realtors he consulted, a young single mom, decided to buy it for herself and her daughter to live in. Allan ran into her about six months after the sale, and she told Allan she had put it up for sale again, informing him that she was selling it because of the ghosts in the house. "They are friendly, but I can't stand them," she said.

In July 2007, both sides of the former Church Street home of Joe and Edith Arndt were purchased by Mill Race, Inc., to become retail properties in the Mill Race Village shopping area. Dave Juliano, director of SJGR, rented 16 Church Street, making it the first official brick-and-mortar home of his already successful online business, the Ghost Hunter Store.

"Mount Holly is a hotbed of ghostly activity," stated Juliano. "It was the place I knew was right for my store." He was so successful in that location that he expanded to 14 Church Street and opened them up into one building to house all of his ghost-hunting products and host seminars and events there.

Seeing his grandparents' house become a paranormal business intrigued Allan Hollowell, so he and Elaine dropped in one day to meet the ghost hunters and welcome them to Mount Holly. SJGR investigator and medium Marti Haines was minding the shop at the time.

Allan introduced himself and Elaine and told Marti he had lived there as a child with his grandparents. Marti wanted to know about some of the "residents" the Ghost Hunter Store seemed to have. She described a large, long-haired, black-and-white dog that visits. "Oh, that's my grandfather's dog, Kim," Allan told her.

"And there is a man here. I have seen a full body apparition of him, and I sense his name is Joe."

"Well, that would be my grandfather," said Allan, amazed, as she was saying things about his grandfather that rang true and even knew his name. This was the first time he had been in the store and the first time he had met Marti.

Joe has also been caught on the Ghost Hunter Store security camera. Juliano related one of those times. "I got a call from ADT saying our front door had come open," he remembered. The police had been called, and they confirmed the door was locked.

Then, ADT told Dave that the alarm had been reset. "But nobody was there; the cops were outside, and nobody had come in. I was on my computer at home at the time and could see the computer in the store was activated, so I turned on the cameras and I saw him standing there." It was a full body apparition of Allan Hollowell's grandfather Joe Arndt. Joe's voice is also often picked up as EVPs on their recorders.

Marti said there are spirits of children in the store, too. There are little boys who hang out mostly on the second floor. There is a little girl who seems to be playing with games or toys. Dave has seen her playing with trigger props on the first floor, probably because they look like toys to her. The Ghost Hunter Store sells paranormal trigger props that look like toy trains or teddy bears and are used to prompt paranormal manifestation. Their

At 16 Church Street, the hunters have been hunted by the prey. *Photo by Judy Gauntt.*

website describes how these toy-like tools work. The concept is that you give the entity something it can identify with. These props are wired with EMF sensitivity alarms that pick up the magnetic field of people and/or entities. Alarm sounds at a variety of distances, ranging from six to twelve inches depending on the magnetic field, but are usually around six inches away.[9]

Up on the third floor, there is a child's handprint on the window. Marti cleans it off, and it keeps coming back. Remember that translucent orb that

Allan saw floating at about a child's height through his grandparent's house, fifty-some years ago? Could it have been one of these children? Who are they? Marti senses they are brother and sister.

And then there's Mary. She would not be happy about fingerprints on window panes. "Mary is the head mistress," said Dave. "She wants it tidy and clean, and she won't stand for disrespect." When Marti described the Mary that haunts the store, Allan told Marti that there was a renter in 16 named Mary years ago and said she fit the description of the ghost.

"If somebody comes in here and makes silly ghost noises and laughs at what we do, Mary throws a flashlight at them. I mean, the flashlight literally is lifted off the shelf, like somebody is picking it up, and then it is flung at the ridiculer," said Marti.

Dave has seen Mary throw the flashlight, too. He said she also used to light some of the religious candles that they sell. "I called Marti because I thought she left them on. But she didn't. We realized it was Mary. I asked her not to do it anymore, and she stopped."

In a back room on the first floor, there is a statue of a bride, a ghostly looking figure in a white dress. This statue moves around the room by itself. They always find it in a different place. When nobody is here, it will move to the middle of the floor or the other side of the room.

When working at the store, staff members often hear people throughout the store, coming from rooms they know are unoccupied. "Every day there is something going on here," said Juliano. "Some days you will see something, other days you just hear voices. Whatever room you are in, you hear voices coming from the other parts of the building, or you hear people running around. I always hear a man and a woman arguing. I go to where the voices are coming from, and there's nobody there."

One time, the neighbors heard the arguing and called the police. The police came and even they heard the screaming, but there was nobody there. All the doors were locked, and no alarms had gone off. The police said the voices were coming from the second floor. So SJGR had another paranormal research group, who knew nothing about the building, come in and investigate.

"They released some spirits, and the grumpy ghost up on the third floor collected them. That's why we refer to him as 'the Collector,'" explained Marti about another ghostly male resident. "We made an arrangement with him that he stay on the third floor because he is so grumpy, and he seems OK with it. Also, sometimes transient energy is attracted here, I guess because they know we are ghost hunters. So the Collector often collects them, too."

"We've asked them if they would like to be someplace else and told them we would help them move on, if they would like. But they all seem happy here and want to stay," said Marti.

"One day a group of kids came in here because they wanted to start a ghost hunting group. One of them saw Mary float by, and they got scared and left. We haven't seen them since," laughed Marti. And they never even saw the others, like the guy everybody sees standing in front of the second-floor bathroom on the 14 Church side. That doorknob also often jiggles by itself, and lights frequently go off and on when nobody is there.

Marti said that SJGR has a piece of equipment that filters out background noise so you can more clearly hear the voice of the spirits. "We had it hooked to a recorder, and we heard a male and female voice talking. We heard the male clearly say, 'I think they know we are ghosts.'"

"I couldn't have planned better," mused Juliano. "A ghost hunter store in a haunted place."

8

BEING WATCHED AT
THE WATCH CASE TOWER

I'm very proud of my gold pocket watch.
My grandfather, on his deathbed, sold me this watch.
—Woody Allen

Thirteen miles north of Philadelphia, where the Rancocas Creek meets the Delaware River, sits Riverside, New Jersey. A farming community settled mostly by German immigrants, it was incorporated as the town of "Progress" in 1851 by a wealthy land developer named Samuel Bechtold. In 1852, Bechtold built the Pavilion Hotel in the center of town. Soon, the beautiful, rural town of Progress between the two lovely waterways became a resort destination for city dwellers from New York and Philadelphia. It was easy to get there by steamship or train, due to its proximity to the river and the Camden-Amboy rail line, which ran along the river, much like today's Trenton-Camden River Line light rail train. Progress became such a hot vacation spot that three other hotels were built, and the tourism business was bolstered by local industry, building a strong economic base for the area. Progress seemed like the right name for the booming town.

Meanwhile, a Swiss youngster named Theophilus Zurbrugg emigrated with his family from Berne to Mount Holly in 1876. His father was a watch case maker, and he opened a small shop in Mount Holly. Theophilus quickly learned his father's trade and soon got a job working for a watch case company in Philadelphia. Business was booming due to advances in gold plating that made watch cases more durable and affordable. A quick learner and astute businessman, young Zurbrugg found himself at the helm of his own watch case company in 1883, when he was just twenty-three years old. He first self-titled his business T. Zurbrugg and Company but later changed it to the Philadelphia Watch Case Company. Starting out as a one-room operation, by the beginning of the next decade, the company had expanded, as Zurbrugg acquired several other watch case companies and upgraded the facilities to a huge factory standing on four acres on Nineteenth Street in Philadelphia.[10]

Back in Burlington County, Bechtold's Pavilion Hotel was not so successful. Bechtold himself died in 1848, while his hotel was still booked solid every summer,[11] but the next decade saw the completion of the Philadelphia–Atlantic City railway, causing the Pavilion's former vacation clientele to take off for the Jersey shore. The Pavilion Hotel, and the resort business in Progress, was floundering.

The visionary Zurbrugg purchased the vacant Pavilion Hotel in 1892 and moved part of his Philadelphia Watch Case Company into it. Then, in order to provide his vastly expanding company a steady supply of resources, he founded Riverside Metal Works in December 1900. From 1892 to 1904, he acquired thirty-nine properties in this small town,[12] which had since changed its name to Riverside. Zurbrugg's decision to move his business here would eventually transform Riverside, as he acquired companies just as he acquired land in the area and became a major employer. He purchased properties to house his employees, including the Homestead, which rented rooms to female employees. He purchased and combined several watch case companies into the Keystone Watch Case Company, and in 1906, as president of the Keystone Watch Case Company, Zurbrugg announced plans to construct a new building adjacent to the Pavilion Hotel to house its operations.

"Every part of this building was made on site," proclaimed Bob Rossi, who today is responsible for the maintenance of the Watch Case Tower, as the building is commonly known. "They mixed the cement right here. The walls are brick and concrete. The ceiling is metal lathe and plaster." Huge cement columns on every floor lend support for this magnificent structure.

In 1908, construction was complete. The ornate, seven-story Victorian building sitting prominently at 1 North Pavilion Avenue, in the center of Riverside, boasts an eight-story tower at the front, which is topped off by an elaborately framed clock on each side. The offices were housed in the front of the building, and the factory, which once employed over one thousand workers producing six thousand watch cases every day, was behind and attached to the office area.

Above: Workers enjoyed a good life in Riverside and earned a decent living at the Keystone Watch Case Company. Have some returned, seeking out old colleagues? *Photo courtesy of the Riverside Historical Society.*

Opposite: The Keystone Watch Case Company building, seven stories built completely on site, has stood in the center of Riverside since 1908. *Photo by Steve Hightower.*

Like Zurbrugg's watches, the Keystone Watch Case Company factory was built to last. But we know nothing lasts forever, and while this landmark structure still stands at Pavilion and Lafayette Streets in the center of Riverside and is still lovingly referred to by many as the "Magnificent Time Piece,"[13] the Pavilion Hotel behind it is gone and, except for the first two floors, the Keystone Watch Case building is vacant—or so it is said.

Theophilus Zurbrugg succumbed to a stroke on November 20, 1912. He is buried in the Mount Holly Cemetery, having been transported there by what was remembered by his contemporaries as the first automotive funeral in the area.[14] He left behind several bequests to his community of Riverside, including a $250,000 trust to fund a hospital, which was opened in the mansion that was the first home to him and his wife, Lisette, when they had moved there.[15]

While Zurbrugg's passing was a blow to the Keystone Watch Case Company, the company continued for a time. It was the introduction of the wrist watch in the 1920s and the subsequent Great Depression that really did the company in. Then, World War II created a shortage of metal for watch cases, as Riverside metal churned out war supplies over watch cases. In 1954, Riverside Metals was sold, and in 1956 the Keystone Watch Case Company was liquidated. The prosperity that Zurbrugg had created was as dead as he was.

While listed on the National Register of Historic Places, the Watch Case Tower building today is but a skeleton of what it was a century ago. The building is now owned by Lippincott Jacobs Consulting Engineers (LJCE), which has renovated the first floor, where the business has been headquartered since 1987. It lends the second floor to the Riverside Historical Society, where the society maintains its office and a museum, which houses over one thousand photographs of historic Riverside. And while the rest of the building lies vacant, many think the historic structure retains some other inhabitants, possibly left there from Zurbrugg's era.

Even though the top five floors of the Watch Case Tower are now vacant, Bob Rossi proudly points out that there are no cracks or structural flaws in its entire seven stories. The ornate elevator shaft still stands, although the elevator that used to transport workers to their jobs every day over one hundred years ago is no longer operational.

A former general contractor and real estate salesman, Rossi has lived in the area his whole life. His great-grandparents were born here, and his maternal grandmother used to work for Zurbrugg making watch cases. Talking to Bob, you can tell he feels great affection for this grand building, which he has

Above: The Riverside Historical Society and Museum reside on the second floor and display memorabilia of Progress and Riverside. *Photo by Steve Hightower.*

Left: This ornate but abandoned elevator once transported workers to their stations every day. *Photo by Steve Hightower.*

been taking care of for the past several years. He also feels there is something in the building that is watching out for him.

Bob's office is in the basement of the Watch Case Tower. A door down in the basement near his office frequently opens all by itself. He will lock it and then sometimes finds it has opened. Bob knows that something is here doing this and believes it is paranormal. "But it is not scary haunted or anything. There is nothing harmful here."

"There is an entity here that helps me," Bob explained. He often works through the night, and he feels that he has a spirit companion. Although he is not positive if it is male or female, he stated, "She doesn't like when I curse."

One night he was working up on the vacant sixth floor. He had a lamp plugged into an outlet in the wall. He inadvertently muttered an obscenity, and suddenly, all by itself, the plug from the light came out of the wall. He checked the prongs on the plug, and there was nothing wrong with them. And it didn't just fall out of the plug, anyway. It was in the outlet tight and came out as if someone had yanked it out. He plugged the lamp back in, and it didn't happen again until he uttered another curse word.

Could it be his grandmother, who worked in this building, chastising him for swearing? "No, I don't believe she is the ghost," he contends.

Strange things happen on floors that are supposedly vacant. *Photo by Steve Hightower.*

The skeletal remains of an office in the Watch Case Tower. *Photo by Steve Hightower.*

This ghostly assistant also helped him one day when it was raining. Some drops of water were dripping through the ceiling. Bob had a bucket on wheels not far from the leak and was going to move it under the drip. But before he could get there, his "assistant" rolled the bucket under the leak; yes, the bucket moved to the precise spot of the drip, all by itself!

While Rossi's dog, a Norwegian Elkhound who is usually afraid of nothing, will not go upstairs in the building, Rossi knows this ghost is really nothing to be afraid of. "I walk throughout this building, up 160 steps across all seven floors. I don't know how to describe it, but I just know this entity is always with me and kind of looks out for me."

Alice Smith, president of the Riverside Historical Society, claims she has never seen anything paranormal, but she has heard some unexplained sounds. And she has been with others when they have heard or seen strange activity. One of these incidents happened when she was with Steve Hightower, an active volunteer with the organization.

The Riverside Historical Society Museum occupies the center of the second floor, extending into other rooms across the hall from the offices. One of these rooms is dedicated to Zurbrugg Hospital, and another room adjacent to that is referred to as the War Room. The War Room honors those Riverside residents who have served our country, and many photos and artifacts are displayed. A couple years ago, somebody had donated pieces of old military uniforms to the Riverside Historical Society Museum. Steve was in the office then, and Alice showed the new additions to him and asked if he would take them over to the War Room and display them.

"There isn't much table space in the war room, and the other shirts and jackets are on hangers bordering the wall. When I got to the room, I stood there momentarily pondering what to do with the items. Out of the corner of my eye, I saw Alice walk by, near the table in the center of the museum, as if she were going towards the bathroom or the rear of the museum." This was only a few steps from the door of the War Room.

"As she walked by, I asked her if we had any additional hangers. Not hearing any reply, I walked to the door to re-ask the question. When I looked into the museum, there was no sign of Alice." He called to her, and she answered from the office, where she'd been all along.

"When Alice emerged from the office, I asked her if she just walked by in that direction, motioning from right to left. She said no and that she'd been in the office for some time. I told her the story of how I just saw somebody walk by and, thinking it was her, asked a question."

The War Room display in the museum honors those of Riverside who served our country. *Photo by Steve Hightower.*

Steve has seen lights in the building dim and flicker for no apparent reason, a common sign of paranormal presence, but this one experience, which was so real and so awesome to him, is the only one he will truly chalk up to a paranormal experience. "I think of myself as receptive to experiences and spirits and have had many of what I believe to be 'paranormal' experiences, but, oddly enough, that is the only one at the Watch Case."

South Jersey Ghost Research investigated the Watch Case Tower on May 31, 1999. The group found evidence of paranormal activity throughout the building. Positive photos of orbs were taken on various floors, especially the elevator shaft, near the main entrance and throughout the unoccupied floors.

"Zurbrugg was good to his workers," stated Bob Rossi. "They enjoyed a good life, living in Riverside at the time and working for him for a decent wage. There were thousands of workers here over time, and maybe this is just where they meet to come together again and remember good times"—magnificent times, maybe, at the Magnificent Time Piece.

9

A Bridge to the Other Side

Hauntings in Roebling

A bridge has no allegiance to either side.
—*Les Coleman, British author and artist*

In 1861, Abraham Lincoln passed through Trenton, New Jersey, calling for volunteers to keep the Union together as Confederate soldiers had recently taken Fort Sumter, igniting the American Civil War. In the crowd was young Washington Augustus Roebling, eldest son of John A. Roebling, the foremost civil engineer in American history. Like his younger brother, Charles, Washington Roebling had been educated at Rensselaer Polytechnic Institute, among other prominent engineering schools, and since finishing his education, he had worked for the family business building bridges. But Washington Roebling signed up the next day as a private for the Union army.

It didn't take long for the young Roebling's engineering skills to be recognized by the Union command, and he was soon promoted through the ranks as an engineering officer. While serving under General McDowell, he was charged with planning and overseeing the construction of military bridges. He designed adaptable bridges and gathered all the necessary building materials so that a bridge could be constructed at a moment's notice. His military projects included a bridge at the Rappahannock River in eastern Virginia and another on the Shenandoah River at Harpers Ferry. He also wrote and illustrated a manual on suspension bridge building for his comrades to use. But it was at the bloody fields of Gettysburg that Washington Roebling's contributions may have had the biggest impact.

This 124-ton, twenty-eight-foot inertial flywheel generated energy for the blooming mill, manufacturing molten steel ingots. What energy remains here from that great industrial time? *Photo by Chris Rein.*

The young Roebling was the first to spot the advancement of Robert E. Lee's troops while flying a hot air balloon on a sunny morning in June 1863. At the time, Roebling was serving under General Warren, who immediately ordered the reinforcement of Little Round Top. But it was soon realized that that no one in the Union command had a detailed topographical map of Pennsylvania. While both armies were en route, Roebling went home to Trenton to get a map that he knew his father had. Riding through enemy territory at night, he reached General Meade by the morning of the first day of combat and delivered the map. Roebling was present at the Battle of Little Round Top and was with General Warren when the Confederates' plans to flank the Union position were discovered. Then a lieutenant, Roebling helped move cannon into place by hand, holding back the Confederates. Many attribute the actions of General Warren's men on that day as the turning point of the Civil War. Thus, after being inspired by Lincoln's speech in Trenton two years earlier, Roebling's participation actively led to the preservation of the Union.

On January 1, 1865, Washington Roebling was given an honorable discharge and retired from the army. He returned to his family in New Jersey, but not before marrying his commanding officer's daughter, Emily Warren. He soon joined his father in Cinncinatti and helped him complete the Covington-Cinncinatti Bridge, which spans the Ohio River between Ohio and Kentucky. At 1,057 feet, the Covington-Cincinnati Bridge, renamed the John A. Roebling Suspension Bridge in 1984, was the longest suspension bridge in the world.

The story of the Roeblings is a stunning tale of hard work, education, dedication and embracing opportunity during the latter part of the American Industrial Revolution. Born Johann August Röbling in 1806 in Mühlhausen, Prussia, now part of Germany, John A. Roebling studied engineering in his native land and then immigrated to the United States in 1831. He helped settle the western Pennsylvania town of Saxonburg, where he designed canals to improve river navigation across the state. The companies building the canals relied on hemp rope. Roebling was not impressed with the rope's lack of durability, so he began to experiment with wire rope for cables. In 1842, he received a patent for spinning wire rope. His wire cable would become the cornerstone of the Roebling empire.

Roebling moved his family to Trenton in 1848 and set up business producing twisted wire cable and promoting its many uses. He would come to build many bridges and receive eleven patents for his innovative creations. The calculations for tolerances and other engineering and architectural features that he designed are still being used today, as are his magnificent bridges, which include the Brooklyn Bridge, the Golden Gate Bridge, the George Washington Bridge and the Ben Franklin Bridge.

By the time young Washington Roebling returned to Trenton with his new bride, Emily, his father and brothers had begun the Brooklyn Bridge project. Unfortunately, the senior Roebling would not see its completion. While walking along the East River to determine the location of the bridge's towers, a ferry boat crashed into the bank and his foot was crushed, paralyzing him. He developed tetanus, and he died in 1869 of lockjaw infection, one of the bridge's twenty-seven casualties.

Washington took over as chief engineer, but he would also find himself disabled before the bridge's completion. Working in pressurized wooden cabins, called pneumatic caissons, the workers were able to go under water to build the bridge's foundation. Moving too quickly in and out of these caissons, or spending too much time down there, could result in "caisson sickness," which many know today as "the bends."

A hands-on manager like he was in the military, Washington spent many days alongside his men. Disregarding his own health, he soon found himself paralyzed and losing his eyesight from caisson sickness. His wife, Emily, learned enough engineering from Washington to take over supervision of the bridge, as her husband watched through a telescope from their apartment window. Surviving scandals, deaths and political battles, the Brooklyn Bridge, the dream of John A. Roebling, was finally completed, and Emily Roebling led the celebratory procession across the great span on May 24, 1883.

John A. Roebling's three sons, Washington, Ferdinand and Charles, built their father's company into the empire it became, the world's leading producer of wire rope. Charles and Washington were the highly skilled engineers while Ferdinand focused on the company finances. Competition pushed the Roeblings to manufacture their own steel, and in 1904, the three Roebling brothers purchased over two hundred acres of farmland in northern Burlington County near the Delaware River. Here, they built the Kinkora Works and the adjacent "industrial village" for their workers. The youngest of the three brothers, Charles, is credited with the vision of building the Roebling village. In fact, Charles designed and built the town against the advice of Washington.

"Roebling's" was a family business, and the industrial village was a "family" town, with generations of families working and living there in its 767 brick homes. Each one had a fruit tree in its yard, and each received a new coat of paint and wallpaper every two years. About 70 percent of the resident workers were immigrants, mostly of Eastern European descent. The village was not unlike any other American town. It had its own schools,

The sprawling Roebling industrial village, two hundred acres along the Delaware River, provided homes and livelihoods to thousands. *Photo courtesy of the Hagley Museum in Delaware.*

stores, athletic fields, churches, fourteen legal taverns (as well as a few places dispensing liquor illegally) and other public places common to most towns. It was just as Charles Roebling had envisioned it; his workers were well cared for and close to the plant.

The main gate was a bustling place. Through it passed nearly five thousand workers every day on their way to their jobs in the steel mills. It was originally just a gate when first built in 1905, but in 1907, a building was added to provide security and limited access to the factory grounds. The building became a hub for the community and business operations of the town, as well as the mills. It was where you punched your timecard and received your paycheck. It was where you were first interviewed for your job and where company administration offices were housed. It had an infirmary and medical services, and for things more dire, it also had a jailhouse.

Elex Passternak was a middle-aged Hungarian immigrant who worked and lived in Roebling and was hired to pick up trash in the allies. Elex fancied himself a ladies' man and often took things a little too far, especially after visiting one of the town's many taverns. One such time was in 1939, when he harassed some young women on a Friday night. One woman filed a complaint against him. Elex was thrown in the company slammer to await arraignment the next day. When the guard went to get him in the morning, he found Elex had hanged himself in his cell. The *New Jersey Mirror* printed his obituary on March 9:

While awaiting a hearing on a charge of immorality, Elex Passternak, 50, a laborer, hanged himself in a cell in the Roebling municipal jail on Saturday. Passternak, who had been arrested Friday night on suspicion of annoying young girls, fashioned a noose from his shirt, attached it to a crossbar and jumped from his cot. A police officer discovered his lifeless body dangling in the cell when he prepared to take the prisoner before Recorder Raymond Hughs [sic]. He had been dead several hours. Passternak resided at 230 Fourth Avenue, Roebling. His funeral took place in Trenton on Monday, with burial in St. Stephen's Cemetery. He is survived by his father, a brother and a sister, all of Hungary.[16]

In 1953, the Roeblings sold the business to the Colorado Fuel and Iron Company, which closed the plant in 1974 due to foreign competition. The homes built for workers still stand today, and the historic town of Roebling is now incorporated in Florence Township. Today, a beautiful museum stands at the site of the main gate to the Roebling mills, a tribute to the engineering

The Roebling Museum, where the gate to the mills once stood, memorializes the Roebling industry and those who kept the mills going. *Photo by Chris Rein.*

ingenuity of the Roeblings, the thousands who worked in their mills and lived in the industrial village, their history and their many contributions to the American way of life that still impact our lives today.

"The site had lain fallow for thirty-four years," related Roebling resident George Lengel, a retired history teacher, whose father and grandfather worked in the Roebling mills, as he did himself for many summers while working through college. Then, in 1982, the two-hundred-acre plant became the focus of a Superfund project, and the Environmental Protection Agency declared it off-limits. A past member of the Roebling Museum Board of Directors, Lengel was one of the many activists in Roebling working to preserve the Roebling legacy through the creation of the museum at the main gate.

Before the clean-up began, the location was deemed worthy of national preservation as a historic site. In an August 1997 article in the *Philadelphia Inquirer*, one industrial archaeologist examining the site declared, "It's like an industrial Pompeii." The team that came through prior to the Superfund clean-up to document its historical significance sifted through old drawings and blueprints and studied the plant's many buildings and machines, "looking for ghosts," as one of those analyzing the site described the process. "You can really feel the presence of the place," a worker from the New Jersey Historic Preservation Office stated in the article.[17]

Whether or not "looking for ghosts" and "feeling a presence" is alluding to actual paranormal activity, I am not sure. But George Lengel has heard many reports of ghosts in the museum and the area of the old mills. George remembered that one of the EPA workers said he always saw a face looking out of the second-floor window of one of the old buildings. He told George that three or four of the men "would always see this man looking at us."

One day when a crew came in to demolish one of the old wire mills, they saw a man walking ahead of them enter the building. The foreman yelled at him to leave as they would soon be bringing it down. But he didn't respond. The foreman instructed a couple of his workers to go in and get him out of there. They went in and searched the building, but nobody was there. And as the remainder of the crew had stood outside watching the building, they knew nobody came out, either.

Paul Varga worked in the mills from 1956 to 1974, when they closed, and like Lengel, still lives in Roebling. Also like Lengel, he was a key player in working to establish the Roebling Museum to preserve the memory of this important community, and he still serves on the board of directors. Paul and George were serving together as museum docents one afternoon in 2011 when a woman came in to tour the museum. She paid her admission and then went into the Roebling Room gallery, which stands where the three jail cells were housed in the days of the steel mills and where Elex Passternak spent his last night on earth.

A few minutes later, "she came flying out of there, screaming that she saw a male ghost who was pressuring her," remembered George. Then she turned and ran out of the building. George and Paul watched as she jumped into her car and sped away. They never saw her again.

Lengel and Varga said that there have been other female visitors to the museum who have reported being touched by something while seeing nothing in this same room. Ghost researchers will tell you that spirits tend to maintain the same traits and personality they had in life. It sounds like the overly flirtatious Elex Passternak has certainly not changed much and that this lecherous ghost is still grabbing what he can, without fear of persecution now.

Elex is also a prankster, it seems, or maybe he just gets bored when there are no women around. The museum hosts meetings for many groups in its Roma Bank Media Room, and George would sometimes stay until the meeting was over to lock up. One such time, the building's alarm system wouldn't set. The control panel kept indicating that there was activity in the gallery, again, where the old jail cells used to be. George went over to the gallery and cleaned off the motion sensor, but it still wouldn't reset. He couldn't leave the building unarmed, and he suspected it was Elex. So he tried to reason with him.

"Yo, Elex, knock it off. I've been here all day. I'm a volunteer. Remember when this place had no roof? No heat? Please let me go home," he urged Passternak's spirit. Elex is not such a bad guy; listening to reason, he stopped setting off the motion sensor, and George was then able to set the alarm and go home.

Another time, George was summoned to the building by the Florence Township police at about 2:30 in the morning because something had activated the alarm. When he arrived at the museum, the police were waiting for him outside. George and the two officers entered the building and, upon searching the premises thoroughly, found nobody in there or evidence of any breaking and entering. The police asked George to reset the alarm. He looked at the panel and saw that it was again the gallery where the motion had been detected, and again, it would not reset. So then, in front of two of Florence Township's finest, he had to ask Elex to knock it off and let them go. "They thought I was nuts," he laughed. But after his colloquy with the spirit, he went back over to the panel and was able to reset the alarm. "Let's get out of here," one of the officers said to his partner.

What would Charles Roebling think if he could see what has become of his vision? Paul believes Charles knows what's here because his ghost is here, too. Neighbors often report that the lights go off and on at night in the building when nobody is here. He thinks it could be Charles. This is a brand-new building, "meticulously" restored by the EPA in 2009;[18] there should be no problem with the electrical system. The lights in the bathrooms automatically go off and on when somebody enters, and possibly this is Charles setting them off at night and causing the neighbors to report it. Paul also remembered sitting in the meeting room once where he could see the restrooms. He heard the urinal flush all by itself, and he knew nobody had gone in there. "Charles was always mischievous," he laughed.

The museum did have a paranormal research group in to investigate the building once since its opening. Paul said that while they were there, the bust of Charles Roebling in the meeting room turned blue. Without confirmation from the investigators on exactly what equipment they were using at the time and the circumstances, I am not really sure what could have caused old Charles to turn blue, but it could possibly have been spirit manipulation. It could have been Charles Roebling trying to communicate or make his presence known, but without knowing the details for sure, we must be skeptical and understand that it possibly could have been atmospheric conditions causing a blue reflection.

Another time the motion sensor went off without any apparent provocation was when a Civil War reenactors group had set up an encampment outside the museum. Paul ponders if that could have indicated the presence of Colonel Washington Roebling, whose interest might have

This bust of Charles Roebling turned blue during a paranormal investigation.

been piqued by the reenactors. Was he was looking for some of his old comrades from the Civil War?

Activity has been felt elsewhere in the museum by others. Women working in the office have reported hearing things in the building when it is empty, and Paul has also had trouble with the electric door malfunctioning for no reason, a prank for which he blames Elex.

Thousands of workers came through these gates for decades, going to a sometimes dangerous job. There were casualties here, as there were on Roebling bridge sites. While the Roeblings provided the workers and their families with a decent wage, a good home and a town that contained everything they needed, there were those who walked through those gates some days and never walked out. Some of the Roebling family members themselves gave their lives to this company. Likewise, there are many who lived their entire lives in Roebling, as did their children and children's children, and many happy times were spent here. All of the emotions and memories of life, whether happy or sad, were contained in the mills and in this village.

Of all the Roebling engineering and bridge-building feats, did Charles Roebling ever think he would be engineering a bridge to the afterlife? I doubt it was on his mind then, but is it not surprising that a place that once contained so much life, blood, sweat and tears would always have energy? How could it not?

The Roebling Museum, at 100 Second Street, sits at the gateway to a remarkable point in American history. It is worth a visit to see this intriguing tribute to the Roebling genius and the workers who made their designs a reality. But a word to the ladies: if you go, watch out for Elex!

10

IT TAKES A VILLAGE
TO HAUNT A TOWN

You arrive at a village, and in this calm environment, one starts to hear echo.
—Yannick Noah, French tennis player and musician

Mount Holly's Mill Race Village includes a restoration project that has converted some of the oldest buildings in town into a quaint, artistic shopping and dining district. The village is so named because it is surrounded by the millrace, a branch of the Rancocas Creek, which looks so peaceful as you sit on the patio at the Robins Nest sipping your martini and watching the ducks and geese swim by; but a century ago, the mighty millrace powered mills and foundries in the area.

White Street, running through the center of Mill Race Village, "is probably the oldest street in town, and once composed the town together with the mills and the few surrounding houses,"[19] chronicles Dr. Zachariah Reade in his *History of Mount Holly*, an 1859 account of just about every building in Mount Holly at the time. White Street was named for Josiah White, who owned the Halsey Cotton Mill and built a brick house on the corner of Pine and Church Streets in 1730. Church Street intersects with White in the center of the shopping district.

Near this intersection, at 7 Church Street, stands the former home of Charles Estill. Surmising from Dr. Reade's listings of buildings, the house might have been owned or built by his father, Joseph Estill, who owned and built many homes in the area. Charles Estill, a Civil War veteran, lived there with his wife, Mary, whom he married on March 6, 1856, in Pemberton. The backyard of 7 Church Street goes all the way back to the millrace, and

Welcome to Mount Holly's Mill Race Village, a place to enjoy art, dining, shopping—all in the company of ghosts.

the Estills maintained a garden along the bank. Charles lived nearly all of his life in Mount Holly and was very involved in his community. He served as clerk at the post office, and he was a justice of the peace, secretary of the Burlington County Lyceum of History and Natural Sciences and president of Relief Fire Company in July 1908. Charles and Mary celebrated their golden anniversary with dinner at their home, as reported in the *Philadelphia Inquirer*, on March 9, 1906. Charles Estill and his wife also both died in this home, she on March 3, 1911, and he on March 14, 1914; both were eighty-three at the times of their deaths. His obituary reported that he had been suffering from a lengthy illness when, on a Saturday morning, he gave a gasp and expired while sitting in a chair. His funeral was also held at his home the following Thursday, as reported in the *New Jersey Mirror*.

A little girl, who was the daughter of a White Street neighbor, Samuel Burr, drowned in the rushing waters of the millrace, as reported by Dr. Reade. The year of her death is not included in his report, but based on the writing of his book and newspaper accounts of the Estills, it is probable that she was a contemporary of Charles and Mary Estill and their children and therefore could have frequently been at 7 Church Street.

Coincidently, the ghost of a little girl is haunting 7 Church Street today. This building is now part of the Mill Race Village restoration and has housed the Earth Angel, the Beauty Bar and Tom's Costumes. Since 2010, it has been the home of Rock, Paper, Scissors, an upbeat beauty salon owned by Judy Grove and Camille Ryan, and Jade Alexandra Boutique, a contemporary fashion boutique owned by Judy's daughter, Jade. The little girl is a constant visitor to their shop and often makes her presence known.

"We know we have a young, female spirit upstairs that also goes downstairs. We have all seen her shadow. Her energy is very inquisitive. She has been here since we were getting ready to open," related Judy Grove. "She is playful, and we feel her following us and watching us as if to say, 'Watcha doin'?'"

Camille added, "She has never given off a bad vibe. I think we scare her as much as she scares us."

The energy level seems to step up whenever somebody new comes into the shop, be it a new client, a new employee or a new Mount Holly police officer stopping in to see how things are going. One day, a little girl came into the shop for the first time with her mom, and everybody was making a fuss over her. The little girl ghost must have felt miffed as suddenly a handful of brushes that were in a jar sitting on a shelf flew up toward the ceiling and then spilled to the floor. The jar was located behind a frame on the shelf, and the jar itself fell behind the frame but remained on the shelf. The brushes flew out of the jar, up over the frame and then fell to the floor, as if somebody had picked them up and thrown them up in the air.

Salon Rock, Paper, Scissors—things going on here could make your hair curl! *Photo by Judy Gauntt.*

"I stopped talking to the little girl in the store after that because I knew our ghost was jealous," said Camille.

Mount Holly resident Alicia McShulkis, who is sensitive to spirit activity, seems to have a connection with the little girl. Whenever Alicia comes in for her appointment, things fall off the color bar. "They don't just plop over; they come off like somebody is picking them up," said Judy.

Jackie is Alicia's regular stylist, and they both often sense the little girl ghost's presence during Alicia's visit. One day, they both sensed her standing around pouting. "Somebody's mad at you today," said Alicia.

"I know," Jackie replied. Jackie is sensitive, too, and the fact that they are both open to her presence could be why she likes to hang around when they are together. She also likes to come around when somebody in the shop appears to be agitated. She likes to know what is going on. She often plays with the stylists' hair, maybe imitating what she sees. "Sometimes I just feel somebody pull my hair straight up," said Judy.

Before leaving on Thursday evening, September 26, 2013, Judy cleaned up the restroom and shined the mirror. She then locked up for the night, as she was the last to leave. Early the next morning, she and Camille opened the shop together. As they came through the door, they both heard a sound that was distinctly the sound of the toilet tank lid being lifted and put back in place. Cautiously, they walked across the floor to the restroom, and Judy peeked around the door. Nobody was there. But there on the mirror—the one Judy had just polished the night before when nobody else was left in the shop—was a child's handprint.

The little girl isn't the only spirit haunting 7 Church Street. Judy and Camille sense another spirit presence sometimes. They feel it is a male who is not particularly friendly, and he tends to stay in the basement in the far end of the cellar. Camille gets a creepy feeling when she goes down there to get supplies. "I try not to look, but my eyes always go there," she said. She sees a large shadow near the furnace, and it is quite ominous. "I get the feeling he does not like me invading his space."

The lights flicker a lot down there, so they had the electric system checked. The serviceman confirmed it was all new and nothing was wrong with it. When they asked what could be the cause, without further explanation, he said knowingly, "It's Mount Holly."

"You mean ghosts?" they pressed the issue further. He just shrugged and left.

Camille and Judy summoned SJGR to get some confirmation that what they are experiencing is paranormal. The professional paranormal researchers checked them out and confirmed there is activity. SJGR medium

Marti Haines said some of it might be residual, but there are definitely interactive spirits there, including a young girl. "She likes to play with toys and moves things around."

They found a toy dinosaur in the basement and put it on the steps. Later on, they found it back down in the cellar, though nobody had been around in the meantime. Typical of a little girl, she also moves the nail polish around and plays with the zombie dolls they sometimes have on display.

But the male presence is not happy, as Judy and Camille had suspected. Marti felt the ground in the basement and said it is very sorrowful; possibly someone died there or was very sick. Could it be Charles Estill, who while an active community member during most of his healthy life, was a widowed, lonely shut-in and feebly sick for a long time leading up to his death? SJGR recorded an EVP of a sigh. Perhaps he is weary.

Rock, Paper, Scissors is only one of many haunted buildings in the village. SJGR director Dave Juliano contends that the most haunted building in Mount Holly—maybe even more so than the notorious Burlington County Prison Museum, which attracts paranormal researchers from around the world—is the Thomas Budd House. It stands at 20 White Street on the oldest homestead in town and now home to Finders Keepers. It has been proven by paranormal professionals to be home to at least seven active spirits, including a nasty old groundskeeper and some children, possibly runaway slaves traveling on the Underground Railroad, which went right through the area.

And across from the Thomas Budd House, on the corner of Church and White, is Home Fine Art, a gallery supporting local artists—and local ghosts. Many spirits have been sensed there, including a man in a black suit and fedora and a woman of Eastern European descent, who likes to tidy up and put things in their proper place, which may not be where the artists want them or put them. The gallery has also at times hosted concerts, which have often stirred up spirit activity, leaving some guests to experience sudden cold spots in a room that was otherwise warm.

In 2007, Elaine Hollowell was at Home Fine Art to attend a concert with her sister and her sister's friend. Between sets, Elaine was in the hallway studying a piece of art that she had been admiring. The only other person around was Bill Gee, who managed the music events at the gallery and who is sensitive to spirits and trained in Spiritual Response Therapy (SRT). Elaine felt a person walk up behind her and then stand right next to her. From the corner of her eye, Elaine could see that he was taller than her and had blond, unkempt hair. He looked kind of windblown, wore an old fisherman-type sweater and kept getting closer and closer to her. He was wheezing and gasping, and he kept moving closer, invading her space. He was creeping Elaine out, so she began to move away but wanted to get a better look at him, so as she moved away, she turned to look—poof! Nobody was there! Somebody who had been so large, obtrusive and invading, so overwhelmingly creepy, wheezing and gasping, had just vanished.

Horrified, she turned to Bill. "I think I saw a ghost!" He just shrugged and smiled, knowingly.

"Yeah, you probably did. We have two upstairs, and they sometimes come down because they seem to like the music. I've asked them to stay upstairs, but they don't. And they are a problem, too, because we can't keep renters upstairs." He was so matter-of-fact about it, Elaine just stood there with her mouth open.

She got little consolation from her sister or her sister's friend, either. The friend, a hospice nurse, professionally deals with death all the time and is very familiar with ghosts and spiritual happenings that occur around death and dying. "She was very matter-of-fact about it and told me, 'Oh, yeah, that's how they talk to you. That sound he made means he was trying to communicate with you,'" Elaine related. Thankful for the beginning of the second set, Elaine tried to focus on the music.

Also at the intersection of White and Church, at 14 White, is the Spirit of Christmas, maybe aptly named for more than the owner's favorite holiday. The spirit of a former resident, Florence, has been seen there by Jo Colino, the owner, as well as some of her staff. A full apparition of Florence—sans face, but with every other detail, including 1940's-type clothing and perfectly coiffed hair—has appeared in the store on more than one occasion. The ghostly lady has been positively identified by her granddaughter, Bonnie, who came to the store to see what had become of her grandmother's former residence. "Her rocker was in front of the window, and she would rock and look out the window," related Jo from the stories Bonnie has told her. Jo enjoys Flo's company, whose rocker would have been right where Jo's point of sale is today.

So what is it about Mill Race Village that causes spirits to linger? South Jersey Ghost Research can point to many factors, and its location is prime. The oldest section of a very historic town, surrounded by water, can provide fertile ground for hauntings. The water of the millrace once powered industry here and now provides a source of energy that spirits can use to manifest. The historical significance of this area—to Mount Holly, to Burlington County and even nationally—provides both a source and a reason for spirits to linger. There has been so much history played out here as the location has been an early colonial settlement, an important battle in the American Revolution, an active industrial period town and a possible stop on the Underground Railroad, just to name a few. Since the days of the Leni-Lenape Indians and then the early European settlers, people lived here, had jobs here and fought for their country here. Emotional events and locations tend to cause spirits to linger; some can't believe they're dead, and some are clinging to the living to help them find reasons for their deaths.

Every year, Mount Holly hosts the Battle of Iron Works Hill, a Revolutionary War reenactment event. Many are not aware that the Battle of Iron Works Hill was a plan by colonial forces to get the Hessians out of Bordentown so that Washington could march on Trenton and win the battle there. The colonials created a skirmish outside Mount Holly, in nearby Springfield Township, that caught the attention and the ire of Colonel Von Donop, commander of the Hessian forces in Bordentown. Van Donop marched his troops out of Bordentown, fought the colonials in Mount Holly and decided to stay there for Christmas. With the Hessians out of

The millrace branch of the Rancocas, for which the village is named, once powered factories. Could it be generating energy for spirits to manifest?

Bordentown, Washington marched into Trenton and won the battle, which ended up being the turning point of the American Revolution.

During Mount Holly's annual reenactment event in December commemorating this important, but often forgotten, battle, some of the reenactors camp out in the village. The replay of the shoot-off itself goes right down High Street from Garden Street and ends up in Mill Race Village. We know that during the British occupation of Mount Holly in 1776, one of the Hessian soldiers was killed in the basement of the Budd House, and his ghost has been seen, heard and smelled there by almost everyone who has rented that building for their business. But there must be other soldiers who come back for this reunion. "Every year after the reenactment, I see ghostly soldiers marching through the village," said Marti Haines.

The Mill Race Village Arts and Preservation project has breathed new life into many former homes and buildings, converting them into businesses that attract many people to the area. The village is a hub of activity in Mount Holly, and often ghosts like to be around activity and watch living people, especially people doing things they liked to do. Ghosts have no sense of time, so they aren't in a hurry; if they liked art and music during their lives, they probably still do, and they have plenty of time for it now and can find it right here. If they were soldiers, maybe they come back to reunite with those doing what they did, maybe even doing what they did when they died. Sometimes, they reach out for companionship or attention, especially to those they feel might be receptive to them.

Another of the many events held in Mill Race Village is the annual Witches Ball, which is rife with paranormal researchers, artists, occult watchers, witches and just good-time partiers—well, why wouldn't this interest a ghost? And if the attraction is reciprocated by people interested in ghosts, it makes a match made in, well, somewhere between here and heaven, I guess.

11

SMITHVILLE

AN EERIE INDUSTRIAL EMPIRE IN EASTAMPTON

Of all ghosts, the ghosts of our old loves are the worst.
—*Sir Arthur Conan Doyle, creator of Sherlock Holmes*

Hezekiah Bradley (H.B.) Smith came to Shreveville, New Jersey, from Lowell, Massachusetts, in 1865 with one of his wives, Agnes. His intent was to purchase an industrial village, where he could move his manufacturing operation.

H.B. had invented and manufactured woodworking machines in Massachusetts and, after fourteen difficult years, was finally turning a generous profit in this business. He looked to New Jersey for the site of his new plant and chose Shreveville because of its water-powered location along the Rancocas, the calm of the countryside with the proximity of the ports of Philadelphia and New York and its distance from his other wife, Eveline, who lived in Woodstock, Vermont, with their daughter, Ella, and three sons—Elton, Eugene and Edward. Eveline refused to grant H.B. a divorce as he requested, but it didn't seem to deter him from marrying Agnes in Lowell prior to moving with her to New Jersey.

Shreveville was an industrial village that had been built in phases by different owners prior to Smith's acquisition. Located in what is today Eastampton Township, the land was purchased in 1776 by Jacob Parker, who built a dam, a gristmill, a sawmill and a home on the property. The property was known then as Parker's Mills. Parker ended up in bankruptcy, and the mill went through several hands before being purchased in 1831 by two Mansfield Township brothers, Jonathan and Samuel Shreve, who intended to manufacture cotton cloth in the mills. The Shreve brothers purchased an additional seven acres, which they annexed to the village to build workers' housing and a mansion for themselves. They renamed their industrial village Shreveville and eventually expanded it to include a school, a store, a barn and stables and smoke- and slaughterhouses. Shreveville employed over two hundred workers, men and women, and annually grossed over a quarter of a million dollars. The Shreves built a canal between their industrial village and Mount Holly. But a nationwide depression in the 1850s, followed by the Civil War, really hurt the cotton industry, and Shreveville floundered. Both brothers died, and the property went up for sheriff's sale in 1858. Afterward, the village of Shreveville lay abandoned.[20]

When H.B. and Agnes saw Shreveville, they knew they had found the place to create their own ideal industrial village and start a new life together. Smith purchased the property for slightly over $20,000, knowing that there would be a tremendous rebuilding effort since it had been abandoned for so long. H.B. and Agnes added their own touches to the property, and it was soon renamed Smithville. To their mansion, improvements included the addition of a bowling alley, a billiards room and additional servants' quarters. The workers benefitted from new and renovated housing and an opera house, where the H.B. Smith Military Band frequently performed. Smith refurbished the shops and established a foundry and other facilities for machinery production. He also added new barns and stables and purchased additional farmland to expand his farm to be one of the largest in the county. He had a schoolhouse for children up to the eighth grade and a credit union and retail stores for his workers right in the Smithville village. H.B. was known as a very progressive employer, providing training, decent wages and attractive living quarters.

Agnes was by H.B.'s side and a true partner, confidante and advisor in his business. While Agnes was employed as a millworker in Lowell, H.B. had taken a fancy to her and invested heavily in her education. He sent her to finishing school and to Penn Medical College in Philadelphia, where she received a medical degree. She participated in decisions concerning his business and was editor to his weekly trade journal, *New Jersey Mechanic*, which had a national distribution. Agnes also established the Smithville Lyceum, a forum for education and cultural exchange in the village. The lyceum also provided entertainment for workers, including a chance to hear and recite poetry and stories, debate popular issues and listen to music.

How could you leave a home like the Smithville mansion? Apparently, you don't! *Photo by Chas Bastien.*

But Agnes butted heads with H.B.'s son Elton, who moved with his father to New Jersey to work in the village. Elton refused to recognize Agnes as his father's lawful wife. After several run-ins with Agnes, Elton found himself expelled from Smithville within a year, never speaking to his father again. Having chosen to desert his mother to join his father, Elton now was in total exile from both parents.[21] He joined the Merchant Marines, where he served from 1868 to 1878, attaining the rank of captain.

H.B. Smith ran a huge village, industrial complex and farm on the site for over twenty years. He went on to expand his business to include the manufacture of bicycles and tricycles, including the unique American Star Bicycle, invented by George Pressley of Hammonton. The Star was a high-wheel bicycle that had the larger wheel in the back and a smaller, guiding wheel in front, to provide greater stability and steering control. This became one of Smithville's most successful products.

As if that wasn't enough to keep him occupied, Hezekiah Bradley Smith was also elected to the U.S. Congress in 1878. He served only one term, as news of his bigamy was soon uncovered. The news did not hold the limelight for long, probably because Eveline refused to prosecute and H.B. refused to admit guilt. So while his congressional career was short-lived, H.B. did later run for, and win, a seat in the New Jersey Senate in 1883.

He served only one term in the New Jersey Senate, and maybe this was because his zest for life had dimmed by this time. During the bitter cold winter of 1880–81, the Rancocas froze, and much work was halted at the village. Then, Agnes fell ill with uterine cancer, and on January 26, she died in her bedroom with H.B. at her side. Her funeral was held in the village at the opera house on January 29, and she was buried in St. Andrew's cemetery on Pine Street in Mount Holly.

H.B.'s partner, in business and in life, for the past twenty-five years, was gone, and with no other family, he was truly alone. He commissioned an Italian marble statue of Agnes to be placed on a pedestal in her favorite spot in the garden, and he could often be seen mourning there.

He sold off part of the farm. The *New Jersey Mechanic* became limited in scope, and its publication reduced to monthly without Agnes at the helm. H.B. became a little eccentric in some ways. For one thing, he began to collect wild animals for his private zoo, which he set up in the mansion courtyard. He also harnessed one of his moose to a carriage and trained him to pull it. And then, he invited six young women to live at the mansion, and rumors abounded about their roles there.

Since H.B. had assumed he would die first and leave everything to Agnes, he now focused on updating his will. His intention was to leave the company to a board of directors who would establish a school for young mechanics, as he and Agnes had both intended. This would later be contested by his family.

H.B. died six years after Agnes, on November 3, 1887, of pneumonia. He was seventy-one. As per his wishes, he was buried next to Agnes in St. Andrew's cemetery. While it seemed strange that he should demand his coffin be iron and then encased in an iron cage set in concrete, his reasons became more apparent when his son Elton reappeared on the scene and tried to have his father's remains removed to be buried in Vermont. Unsuccessful in this attempt, Elton had more success at contesting his father's will, although it took a decade in court to do so. In 1899, after gaining control of the company, Elton began repairs on the mansion. One of the first of his improvements was to have the statue of Agnes removed from its garden pedestal, smashed to fragments and the shards thrown into the deep and swift Rancocas.

The H.B. Smith Machine Company thrived under second- and third-generation Smiths for several decades, even constructing a "bicycle railway" between Smithville and Mount Holly for commuting workers, but the Great Depression saw the end to prosperity there. Descendants of the Smith family continued to occupy the grounds into the 1960s.

Before the county purchased the property in 1975 to make it the first Burlington County park, Hilda Smith, daughter of Captain Elton Smith, had a meeting with Ben Cook of Cook Realty in Hainesport to meet a prospective buyer. She was told that Mr. Hugh Heffner would be arriving to meet her, dressed for high tea, and that she should dress appropriately. During their meeting, Hilda pressed Mr. Heffner about what he did for a living, and he daftly avoided the subject. Fed up with his evasiveness, Hilda stood up and said to the two men, "You can show yourselves out, gentlemen." The meeting, and any prospective real estate deal, was over.

Today, the mansion, annex and village are listed on both the New Jersey and the National Registers of Historic places, and Smithville Park is a beautiful place for hiking and picnics. Tours of the mansion are available, and the site is home to many cultural and seasonal events. It is also home to many spirits, according to investigators and mediums from both SJGR and South Jersey Paranormal Research (SJPR), as well as many volunteers and docents who work at the mansion. SJGR conducted nine investigations there over a two-year period in 2006 and 2007, and SJPR was there twice in 2007. Both groups investigated the mansion as well as the barn, schoolhouse and other outbuildings. SJGR reported receiving a higher than average number of positive orbs and EVP recordings during many of its investigations.

"They like to talk," said SJGR's Marti Haines of the spirits at Smithville. "We ask them questions, and they answer us." SJPR investigators seemed to have the same experience, as their case study of their first investigation at Smithville stated, "We have never before captured so many EVPs from one investigation!"[22]

"Oh, we have 'em!' said Larry Gladfelter on being asked if he believes there are spirits in the Smithville mansion. Larry has been involved with the mansion since 1978 and was an acquaintance of H.B.'s granddaughter Hilda. Larry is very familiar with the history of Smithville and the family, and he even sees H.B. himself, often in the family sitting room on the first floor. "He just sits in the chair and looks at you," Larry said. H.B. also likes to sit near the organ when it is in use.

Of H.B., SJGR's Marti Haines said, "He is a little grumpy, and he wants to be addressed as 'Mr. Smith,' not by his first name. You know when he is there. Sometimes he will interact, but he is kind of withdrawn."

SJPR investigators found old H.B. to be a little more commanding. When one of them was in the room H.B. had used as an office, she captured his booming voice saying, "Dust off the book!"

Agnes and H.B.'s bedrooms were adjoined by an archway between them. "The male ghost hunters felt they were pushed towards his bedroom, while the women felt they were pulled towards hers. It was like we weren't supposed to be in the other room," remarked Marti. SJPR also reported that in the bedroom with the male presence, the female researchers felt they were not welcome.

Elton is often at the mansion. Both Jo and Larry have seen him in the double parlor. "The room gets colder when he is present," said Larry. "He is often brooding. But he was a big man, about 6'4" and 300 pounds. He was not abusive, but his children were a little afraid of him, probably because of his size."

"His wife was a little harsh," reported Jo Stepler. "When SJGR was here, her spirit told us to go outside. She said there was more activity out there, anyway."

And maybe she was right. The schoolhouse, where many workers' children were educated, is especially active. SJGR picked up on children's voices, a male in the attic, somebody who is a teacher or schoolmaster and a little girl. They heard footsteps upstairs, and the EMF meters constantly went off, indicating fluctuations in energy fields and the presence of spirits. SJPR also captured many EVPs of male and female voices throughout the schoolhouse. Some definitely seemed interactive, reacting to what they were doing. For example, when one investigator took a picture in the direction of another investigator, an EVP was captured saying, "Isn't he pretty?"

During the SJGR investigation conducted on May 19, 2007, one investigator sang a couple lines of the Kenny Rodger's song "The Gambler" to herself. Right then, the investigator working with her captured an EVP that said, "Don't sing."[23]

Most spirit activity that seemed to come from children was in the annex. "If you go into the bowling alley, in the annex, there is a lot of activity," said Marti. In these areas, many investigators recorded spirit voices, and often they captured photos of orbs at the same time their motion detectors went off. SJPR also felt a male presence keeping an eye on them in the bowling alley.

On one investigation, Marti encountered Billy, sitting on a garden bench. Marti sat down next to him. He told Marti that he was a great-grandson of Hezekiah B. Smith. He told her that H.B. kept animals on the grounds, wild animals like elk and giraffes and a full herd of reindeer.

Bedrooms in the mansion, dressed up for the annual holiday tour.

Marti then noticed a moose standing behind a nearby tree, with a huge, full rack. At the time of this investigation, Marti was not aware of H.B. Smith's collection of wild animals or the fact that he had moose, one of which he had harnessed to draw his carriage. Before Billy "left," he told Marti he was "thrilled about the plaque" somebody had placed on his bench. She then noticed a bronze plaque affixed to the bench she had just shared with Billy. It reads:

In Memory Of
Justin Allen "Billy" Pie, LT., USA
Killed In Action WWII
Great Grandson of Hezekiah B. Smith

Another time Marti was there, she saw Billy standing at a window in the dining room of the annex, looking out into the backyard at his plaque. Many others have reported seeing Billy looking out that window; one investigator said she saw him looking out the window with tears in his eyes. Larry Gladfelter said he often sees Billy at the back door. Billy likes to whistle and call out, "It is I!"

In the barn, the investigators heard the sounds of hoofs and a horse whinny. Marti said she thinks that is mostly residual energy. Residual energy is different from the interactive energy they were picking up in other parts of the Smithville Village. Residual energy means that the spirits are not earthbound, and there will be no interaction between you and them. Their energy remains there from the past, and if conditions are right, you will see it play before you, much like a video playback.

Joyce Wright, a member of the Friends of the Mansion and a docent there for tours, said that things just seem to disappear or get moved around quite frequently. One time, they were looking for some sconces that had been stored on the third floor. Several of the volunteers searched for these sconces; they all knew exactly where they should be. They searched for a year before they just gave up. Then one day, Joyce went up on the third floor, and there they were, right where they were supposed to be. Many volunteers and employees had walked by that spot on various occasions, and they had not been there. "Nobody knows [why they happen]," she said of the strange things that go on in the mansion.

Larry Gladfelter often leads candlelight tours of the mansion during the holidays. At 9:00 p.m., when he usually has his group upstairs, they will often hear a loud "bang," as the shutters on the first floor slam shut.

Billy is pleased with the bench dedicated to his honor.

"That would be Fritzie Gsell," he laughed. Fritzie was H.B.'s gardener, and at 9:00 p.m., it was his job to shutter the first floor of the mansion for warmth and security.

Jo Stepler, also a Friend member and docent at the mansion, has had many encounters and has been there when paranormal researchers and others have encountered spirits. One time in 2011 when she was conducting house tours of the mansion, a twelve-year-old girl came in with her mother. The young girl told Jo there was a man outside by a tree in the yard, and he was pointing and laughing at her. He told her that he could not go in because the woman in there wouldn't let him. Jo looked out but didn't see anyone there. The girl's mother told Jo that her daughter was a medium and could see people that others could not see.

"Who is the man?" Jo asked the girl.

"His name is Elton," the girl replied. "He said that Agnes won't let him come upstairs."

Jo had never seen this girl or her mother before. They were a military family, stationed at Maguire Air Force Base. Jo was shocked. The mother said that she, herself, could sometimes feel things but that her daughter actually

103

had the ability to see spirits and people from the past. About ten minutes later, Jo was near the double parlor and heard "bang, bang, bang!" coming from the staircase. It was the young girl, running down the steps. Agnes had chased her out of her bedroom because she saw the girl glance into H.B.'s room. "Don't look in his room!" Agnes had scolded her.

The girl felt pressure in the hallway by the back steps. "Somebody fell down here," she told Jo.

"Yes, my husband did when he was trying to wipe up a spilled drink," Jo informed her.

"Agnes pushed him," the girl said. Apparently, Agnes was not so fond of men.

Others have been pushed around at the mansion. One time when SJGR was there, one of the male investigators felt a shove. "Are you trying to push me?" he asked. When the recording from the investigation was played back, they heard an EVP response that said, "Yeah" with a laugh.

Jo said that some investigators have encountered spirits that predate H.B. and Agnes. One encountered the spirit of a young girl named Becky. Jo's husband researched who that could be and found that Rebecca Shreve lived there before the mansion was bought by H.B. and Agnes.

Hezekiah Bradley Smith, an eccentric and brilliant man, and his beloved partner, Agnes Wilkerson Smith, would probably want you to enjoy your time at beautiful Smithville Park. They influenced the lives of many in the area. They were fair to their workers, and they created products that made a difference in the world. Their village was unique and progressive while their own residence was grand. And since he is still there, please give a nod of thanks to the man who built this empire and left us a legacy that we can all enjoy. Despite the vengeance of Elton, H.B.'s legacy lives on to educate us and provide us a place for culture and recreation, just as he provided to his employees. In a way, the intent of his will has been satisfied; after all, he and Agnes rest in nearby Mount Holly together, something Elton was not able to change, either.

"The atmosphere was always pleasant there whenever we investigated," said Marti, probably an indication that H.B. is pleased with what has become of his homestead and the industrial village he built. Just don't incur the ire of Agnes!

12

LET'S MAKE A DEAL

Let us never negotiate out of fear. But let us never fear to negotiate.
—John F. Kennedy

I believe my job is to get tormented spirits to the white light. They often don't know they are dead, especially if they have died suddenly. Or if they have suffered for a long time before they died, they may have left unfinished business on earth and, therefore, find it difficult to cross over. I encourage them to do so, to go to the white light. I remind them they have family members on the other side who are waiting for them."

Jeannie Francis is a lifelong resident of Burlington County, a medium and a paranormal investigator, all of which she does in addition to her Palymra-based reflexology and herbalist business, Spirit to Sole Connection. She often leads ghost investigations and informational seminars on spirits and understanding them.

"If a homeowner is feeling tormented by what seems to be paranormal activity in their home, it is often because the spirit is just trying to communicate with them and [is] mustering up all [its] energy to get their attention," she goes on to explain. Spirits need energy to manifest and often take that energy from the electricity in the home or nearby water sources. It is not often easy for them to generate enough energy to manifest, so sometimes they might seem grumpy, especially if you don't respond.

Jeannie often likes to form agreements with spirits that cohabitate with homeowners, coming to a resolution that is satisfactory to both the homeowner and the ghost. She tells a story of a ghost that was becoming a nuisance in a friend's home in nearby Riverton, near the Riverton Country Club. Jeannie helped her friend and the spirit form what she likes to call "a ladies' agreement."

Her friend Susan had purchased this lovely home but soon came to realize she and her husband were not alone in their new abode. They would find things moved from one place to another (when neither of them had touched these objects), glasses would fall off a table by themselves and break, lights would blink and other abnormalities occurred. The spirit was trying very hard to make itself known and took to frightening company who visited the couple or clients who came to Susan's home-based business.

Finally, Susan had enough and asked Jeannie if she would come over and give her a hand with this unruly ghost. When Jeannie visited, she told Susan that she had a strong feeling this was a female ghost and that her name was Susan, also. Then Jeannie, a member of the both the Riverton and Riverside Historical Societies, researched the history of the house and found that it had been built as a wedding gift for a woman whose name was, indeed, Susan. It seemed very likely that whoever was haunting the house was a little miffed that another woman now ruled her beloved earthly home and even had the nerve to have her name! Would the new Susan take her place as the prominent Lady Susan of this beautiful home?

So Jeannie told her friend that she would be back. They agreed on a date, and Jeannie told her to have three glasses of ice tea ready, as they were going to sit down and work out a ladies' agreement with the ghost.

On the day of the meeting, the two friends sat down, and Jeannie summoned the ghostly Susan and invited her to join them, letting her know that the other glass of tea had been poured for her. Jeannie spoke to both Susans, trying to explain and work through the situation.

She assured Susan (the ghost) that, yes, the home was originally hers and it was understood how much she loved her home and how hard it must be for her to see another woman keeping the house, especially one who shared the same first name. But time has moved on, and she needs to understand that. She told the ghostly Susan that she was indeed welcome to stay here, but she must not play tricks or frighten people because that is unkind. The new Susan agreed and let her predecessor know that she was still welcome here.

They then also told the ghostly Susan that she could even have her own room in the house. They chose a room on the top floor that Jeannie sensed had been one of her favorites. They put a big rocking chair by the window so that the ghostly Susan could sit and look out over the golf course, and they put a table in the room with a light that came on at night. That was about five years ago, as of this writing, and the new Susan and her husband have reported no problems since the agreement was reached. But neighbors walking by the house at night often report seeing the rocking chair going back and forth, as if someone were sitting in it, gazing out the window.

Many would agree with Jeannie that befriending and working things out with spirits with which you must cohabitate is the route to take. I'm sure one of the former shop owners of a recent Mount Holly business would concur.

The Thomas Budd House in Mount Holly is a brick, colonial-style, two-and-a-half-story home that has stood at 20 White Street since 1744, the oldest known dwelling on its original site in town.

Budd's old house has been the home of several businesses in the past decade and a half. For two years, around 2005, it housed Uniquely Native, a shop selling scented candles, handmade basketry and Native American

The Thomas Budd House, the oldest Mount Holly dwelling on its original site, is believed by some to be the most haunted building in town.

jewelry and art. It was owned by Mary Carty and Cathy "Starfire Woman" Chadwick-Ciccone, both of Native American descent.

Cathy is a full-blooded Leni-Lenape and would often listen to her native music while working in the shop. But soon she began to experience a problem with the music. CDs that worked perfectly fine began to skip like crazy, but not all of them. Sometimes, the stereo would even shut off, and occasionally, it would turn on and then off again. This made no sense at all, as the CDs worked fine in her home and car and the stereo was new. Several customers witnessed the phenomenon, as well. Cathy even took the stereo home and played the same CDs, but it never skipped outside the shop.

Then one day, Cathy realized the phenomenon occurred only when certain Native American "vocables" were played, never during any other type of music. Cathy explained "vocables" as "native vocalizations, without words, such as 'wey-ya-hey-ya,' often using a high-pitched voice, repeatedly, almost like a wail. It is an older, more traditional type of native music." Cathy and Mary knew the shop was haunted, as they had had many experiences, and now Cathy realized that maybe the spirits were objecting to this particular music. So Cathy decided it might be time to smoke the peace pipe and come to an agreement they could both live with.

"OK, you don't like my music. I get it. I probably wouldn't like yours either. We need to come to an agreement," she began to negotiate with them. "I'll make a deal with you. We'll take the days; you can have the nights. I think that's fair." She stopped playing the vocables whenever she stayed to work late at the shop at night, and the stereo stopped malfunctioning during the daytime. Mutually agreeable terms had been struck, and Cathy and the spirits of the Thomas Budd House lived on in harmony.

Not far away, at 41 Union Street in Mount Holly's historic district, sits a large, uniquely styled home with a third-floor walkout porch. It has balustrades, turned posts and a gabled roof and was originally the residence of Craig Moffett, a Mount Holly pharmacist. Moffett was born in Burlington City in 1846. He bought the Union Street lot and had his spectacular house built in 1885, where he only had a short walk to his pharmacy around the corner on High Street.

Moffett's wife was named Elizabeth, and they had two daughters—Louisa and Elizabeth. Their only son, Craig, died in infancy. Being faithful parishioners of St. Andrews Episcopal Church, they buried Craig Jr. in St. Andrew's Cemetery, on Pine Street, where the entire family now rests.

Around 1905, Craig Moffett was diagnosed with stomach cancer, so he sold his pharmacy and retired. He then just stayed home with his wife and

Everybody knew Craig Moffett's house was haunted, except the new owners!

spinster daughters. As his disease progressed, his pain worsened. One day in June 1910, he went back to his old pharmacy and purchased carbolic acid, a toxic fluid chemical, which he said he was going to use to "clean his instruments." He then wandered to a bench in front of the courthouse on High Street, sat down and drank the deadly liquid. When he didn't come home for dinner, one of his daughters went out to look for him and found him, lifeless, on the High Street bench.

As was common at the time, the viewing and funeral were held in his Union Street home. His burial followed at St. Andrews Cemetery. Elizabeth joined him there the following year after suffering a stroke.

Louisa and the younger Elizabeth remained in the Union Street home for the rest of their lives. They were often seen walking around Mount Holly, going to church or to work. They always dressed in black, wore their hair in buns and carried Bibles. Elizabeth predeceased Louisa. When Louisa died on November 26, 1952, she willed the house to St. Andrew's church, fully furnished. In 1954, Edwin Smythe bought it from the church for one dollar.

Around Halloween 2000, Ed and Bonnie Micallef purchased the home from Smythe's daughter, Ann. Ed asked her if anyone had ever died in the house or if it was haunted. "The realtor told me they must disclose ghosts and buried oil tanks in the house," laughed Ed, as he recalled that Ms. Smythe told him no deaths had occurred in the house but that the original owner did take his own life outside the home.

For about a month after the purchase, Ed worked on the house, making renovations and helping move some of Bonnie's furniture and belongings in. All while he was working, he had a strange feeling somebody was watching him, especially up in the attic. He felt extremely uncomfortable and always wanted to leave as soon as he could.

Bonnie moved in over Thanksgiving weekend; Ed was working in Jersey City at the time and so did not move in until early 2001. Bonnie reported that she did not feel the strange eeriness that Ed had experienced, at least not while she was the only one living there.

In 2001, before Ed had taken up residence at the old Moffett estate, Bonnie went on a business trip to China, and Ed stayed in the house. "I started getting those lousy feelings again," he remembered, and he was overcome with a feeling of malaise. So he would start up to bed, and he would hear cracks and creaks and noises coming just from the house itself. He tried to convince himself that the house "was just settling."

Ed got into bed and put the covers over his head. He started feeling pressure like he was being smothered; something was holding him down, and he was gasping for breath. He jumped up and put the lights on, and whatever it was stopped bothering him.

Bonnie returned from China and said she was fine staying alone in the house, and then Ed moved in permanently. That's when the spirits became apparent to both of them.

They had plastic down over a runner in the hallway, and they would both hear footsteps on it at night, coming up the stairs in the wee hours of the morning. They slept with the bedroom door ajar, and the footsteps always stopped in front of the doorway. Then the footsteps often went up the attic steps, and they would hear them walk across the attic floor. They would then return down the attic steps and, again, stop in front of the bedroom doorway.

They were told Ann Smythe never slept in that room. She slept in the back bedroom with her dog and cat.

There was no doubt something was there; they both knew it. After researching the history of the house and the Moffetts, Bonnie and Ed began to understand about the spinster daughters. They figured maybe it was these ladies that were still in the home, and they were very upset about Ed living there and sleeping in the same bed with Bonnie. Bonnie's presence alone didn't seem to bother them; that was life as they knew it, and it seemed they accepted her. But when a man moved in with her, that was another ballgame.

To celebrate their first Christmas living in their new home, Bonnie and Ed invited their families over. "My sister has a thing for seeing the dead," Ed said of his sister, Karen. So while Karen was over, Ed asked her if she saw anything. Karen told him, "There is a man and a woman at the top of the stairs. The woman is wearing her hair in a bun. The man is older, and he looks very sickly."

Having never told his sister anything about the spiritual disturbances they were experiencing or anything at all about the Moffetts, he listened in awe as Karen "described Craig and Louise to a 'T.'" So it was Craig and his daughter, Louise, that remained in the house!

A few months later, it was a spring morning after Easter 2002, and Bonnie and Ed were sitting in their kitchen enjoying their morning coffee. Ed's sister, Karen, had given them a stuffed bunny for an Easter gift, which they had placed on top of the refrigerator. Suddenly, they watched in amazement as the stuffed rabbit, quite by itself, jumped straight up in the air, turned itself upside down and landed on the floor!

Well, that did it. They realized they had to come to terms with the spirits; they could no longer cohabitate like this. They must reassure the spirits and come to an understanding with them, letting them know that their beloved house was in good hands.

Bonnie got up and started walking around the kitchen. "We know you are here," she summoned them. As she walked throughout the house, she continued trying to reason with the ghosts of Craig and Louise Moffett. "Your sister, your wife and your mother are waiting for you. The house is in good hands. We love it, and we'll take care of it. Go to the light. We will pray for you. We are members of St. Andrews, and we have a lot in common with you. We promise we will not change the house you love. It's 2002 now. It's been almost one hundred years, Mr. Moffett. Please, both of you, go; your family is waiting for you!"

Mr. Moffett and his daughter seemed to accept Bonnie's offering, reassurance and encouragement to pass over, as they have not been haunting the house since that spring morning. While there were no more footsteps in the attic or shadows on the wall, no more standing outside their bedroom at three or four o'clock in the morning, there was one more spirit that remained in the house and took a while to go.

One night, Bonnie and Ed were reading in bed. They heard the distinctive sound of cat paws on the plastic-covered runner outside their bedroom door. They didn't think it could be their cat, Billie, as she always stayed in the kitchen at night. The paw steps came to the bedroom door, and then they felt a weight hit the bottom of their bed. They looked toward the foot of the bed and even saw a depression in the bedspread and blankets. They knew a ghost cat had just jumped in bed with them. Then the ghost cat started cuddling up to them. This happened on several occasions, and being cat lovers, this was one ghost they didn't mind! (Good thing, because everybody knows how easy it is to negotiate with a cat!)

Ed's parents house-sat for them several times when they went away, and the ghost cat visited them, too, making Ed's mom very happy. She even caught a glimpse of him, a silver tabby. She tried to go toward him, but he disappeared.

Bonnie also caught glimpses of the tabby; she would be working on her computer and would look up to catch him watching her but then disappear. Billie also sometimes saw the ghost cat. She would stare at him and then open her mouth as if to speak to him. Billie usually doesn't like other cats and tends to just stare them down. But it seemed like she wanted to converse with her ghostly counterpart.

The ghostly tabby hung around for a couple more years, and he was a pleasant companion. But then he left. Bonnie and Ed believe he belonged to the Moffetts and finally crossed over to be with his human family. Dogs often cross over right away if their owners have, but cats sometimes stick around for a while—probably part of their more inquisitive nature or maybe because they have nine lives!

In February 2003, Bonnie and Ed had one more visitor, one whom they knew very well. On a cold night, they stayed home for the evening with the heat cranked up, feeling nice and toasty as they sat on the couch and watched *NCIS*. Suddenly, the air right in front of their faces got artic cold. "Especially my nose; it was like ice," Bonnie remembered.

"It's your father," said Ed. Bonnie's dad, Mr. Luciano Oquendo, had just passed away in December, and a few nights earlier in a dream, Bonnie had seen him cross over.

"Please move, Dad; you are making me cold," requested Bonnie. Ed suggested to Mr. Oquendo that he move to the other couch and watch TV with them. He did. "Just like in life, he lived to please," Bonnie said, as she fondly remembered her dad.

Ed felt the air on the other side of the room, and it was cold, while the rest of the room remained warm. Mr. Oquendo stayed with them for about half an hour, and Bonnie and Ed chatted with him and then he left, as did the cold air. A few nights later, Bonnie dreamt she was having coffee with her father and asked him where a ring she wanted was. Her stepmother had told her the ring was buried with Oquendo, but her dad said that wasn't true; her stepmother had the ring. Bonnie later found out that this was true.

A couple years ago, Bonnie and Ed were chatting to a fellow parishioner at St. Andrews about their paranormal experiences and how Ann Smythe had not disclosed that there were ghosts in the house.

"Everybody knew that house was haunted," laughed their friend, whose family has lived in Mount Holly for many, many years. "That house has been haunted since Craig died. The sisters knew their father was still there. He probably felt guilty about abandoning them and so stayed on to watch over them. The daughters probably never married because they knew their dad was still there."

Bonnie and Ed soon found out that all the other parishioners at their new church seemed to have known the house was haunted, but nobody ever told them. To this day, St. Andrews Episcopal Church still holds masses for Craig Moffett, the former Mount Holly pharmacist who can now rest peacefully, reassured his beloved home is in good hands.

13

SO, THE GHOSTS ARE REAL?

Everything dies, baby, that's a fact
But maybe everything that dies someday comes back
—from "Atlantic City," by Bruce Springsteen

"Spirits are just like people, without the hard shell. They are everywhere. Everyone is born with the capability to see spirits, but as we grow older and get busy, we shut that ability down. You can always learn it again." So said Marti Haines as she began her presentation on ghost hunting at Mount Holly's Thomas Budd House, one of the most haunted buildings in the county seat of Burlington County.

Most mediums and paranormal researchers will tell you that a person's character will likely remain the same after death. So unless you encounter the ghost of Blackbeard, most Burlington County ghosts will not attempt to hurt you. Some might not even be aware of your presence, especially if it is residual energy, but many are quite aware and might even try to get your attention. Some are mischievous, scared or shy. You might smell their pipe tobacco or perfume as they float by you, or they might hide things on you or throw something at you to get you to notice them. You might capture an orb when you take a photo or feel someone tap you when you see no one there. Be open to them; they are everywhere!

On almost any given evening, you will find a group of ghost hunters at the Burlington County Prison Museum in Mount Holly. It is one of the most haunted buildings in the area and has gained international recognition in many books and on the Sci-Fi Channel's popular ghost hunting show

The last earthly home for Joel Clough was this maximum-security cell at the Burlington County Prison. *Photo by Judy Gauntt.*

TAPS. Besides this building's notoriety in the fields of architecture, criminal justice and corrections, it is renowned for the ghosts there, one of the most notorious being Joel Clough, who spent time there before his hanging in 1832 for murdering his girlfriend. Likewise, many other tortured souls spent their final days there, and many remain to haunt the building.

Around Halloween 2013, Eva Hershey of the Mount Holly Historical Society heard about the tormented souls trapped in the prison, especially Clough, and took pity on them. She decided to go over and sing to them, thinking that would bring them some solace. By chance, the day when Eva was there, the door to the solitary confinement cell where Clough spent his final days was open for maintenance. Eva felt a jolt of energy as she neared the cell. She then went inside and sang "Amazing Grace."

"I felt tremendous compassion as I stood in the doorway imagining how terrible that would be. I went in and walked around singing. I sang with the intent of bringing peace to a troubled soul, and it felt good. I continued walking and singing as I felt led," recalled Eva on her first visit to the old prison. She is convinced the ghosts felt her singing and said, "I am interested in creating awareness of ghosts having feelings."

Has Eva's melodies soothed the souls that remain in the old prison? Possibly, but Marisa Bozarth, the museum curator, doesn't think any of them have left. She still feels their presences, and it is still a popular haunt for ghost hunters. "I did have a woman from Browns Mills in recently who was a medium and told me there is a man, probably a guard, who watches over the jail and likes to 'annoy me' by following close behind. I get that feeling a lot, so I thought it was interesting. Also, she said that most of the spirits are not necessarily trapped but more afraid to cross over due to fear of leaving something or someone behind or where they will be going in the afterlife."

See? They are just like us. They play pranks, they have emotions and fears and they are concerned for others. They are even concerned about their future, where they are destined to be in the afterlife. Does it get any more real than that?

NOTES

Chapter 1

1. U.S. Army official website, "America's Haunted Army," http://www.
army.mil/article/13090.

Chapter 2

2. Ellis Parker Tribute.
3. *Nashua Telegraph*, "Hoffman's Detective Arrested."

Chapter 3

4. Revolutionary War New Jersey, "Revolutionary War Sites in Hainesport,
New Jersey."

Chapter 4

5. Mount Holly Library, "History of the Langstaff Mansion."

Chapter 5

6. Judy Olsen, e-mail conversation with the author, April 27, 2013.

Chapter 6

7. SJGR, case notes, June 29, 2007 investigation of Library Company of Burlington, http://www.southjerseyghostresearch.org/cases4/07032.html.

Chapter 7

8. Ledwith and Heinemann, *Orb Project*, 79.
9. GhostHunterStore, http://theghosthunterstore.com/?s=trigger+prop&s_cs=true.

Chapter 8

10. Hidden City Philadelphia, "File Under: Lost Francisville," http://hiddencityphila.org/2012/09/file-under-lost-francisville.
11. Riverside Historical Society website.
12. Frazier, "Keystone Watch Case Company," 6.
13. Weaber, "Decades Old Mystery."
14. Ibid., 21.
15. Zurbrugg Memorial Hospital website.

Chapter 9

16. http://www.bcls.lib.nj.us/newspapers/newjerseymirror/njmirror.phtml.
17. http://articles.philly.com/1997-08-18/news/25567978_1_superfund-plant-buildings-epa.
18. http://roeblingmuseum.org/about-us.

Chapter 10

19. Read, *Read's History of Mount Holly*, 50.

Chapter 11

20. Shreve: The History of an American Family website.
21. Bolger, *Smithville*.
22. SJPR website, http://www.sjpr.org/case-studies/eastampton-nj-april-28-2007.
23. SJGR website, http://www.southjerseyghostresearch.org/cases4/07024.html.

BIBLIOGRAPHY

Bolger, William C. *Smithville: The Result of Enterprise*. Mount Holly, NJ: Burlington County Cultural and Heritage Commission, 1980.

Burlington City Historic District website. http://www.tourburlington.org.

Burlington County website. http://www.co.burlington.nj.us.

"Constance Bennett Dies at 59." Article from July 26, 1965 (original source unknown). http://www.constancebennett.byethost14.com/Articles/Constance%20Bennett%20Dies%20at%2059.htm.

Ellis Parker Tribute. http://www.patfullerton.com/1e/newspaperbio2.html, quoting the *Camden Courier Post*, February 5, 1940.

Frazier, Susan. "Keystone Watch Case Company." Master's thesis. Rutgers University, New Brunswick, NJ, 1997.

Ghost Hunter Store website. www.theghosthunterstore.com.

Hafetz, David. "In Steel Giant's Ruins, History Lives Roebling Steel, a Superfund Site in Florence, Is a Classroom for Now." *Philadelphia Inquirer*, August 18, 1997.

Hainesport Township municipal website. http://www.hainesporttownship.com/about/history.html.

Hidden City Philadelphia website. http://hiddencityphila.org.

Historical Society of Riverton. *Gaslight News*, November, 2008. http://rivertonhistory.com/wp-content/uploads/2010/11/134_Gaslight_News_Nov08.pdf.

History.com. "Brooklyn Bridge." http://www.history.com/topics/brooklyn-bridge.

LaBan, Craig. "Military 'Superclinic' in the Works the Old Walson Army Hospital Is Crumbling. The New Outpatient Facility Will Reflect Trends." *Philadelphia Inquirer*, November 2, 1995.

Ledwith, Miceal, DD, LLD, and Klaus Heinemann, PhD. *The Orb Project*. New York: ATRIA Books, 2007.

Lee, Francis Bazley. *Genealogical and Memorial History of the State of New Jersey*. N.p.: Lewis Historical Publishing Company, 1910.

Library Company of Burlington website. http://www.librarycompanyofburlington.org.

Lippincott Jacobs Consulting Engineers website. http://www.ljce.net.

Mott, A.S. *Ghost Stories of New Jersey*. Auburn, WA: Lone Pine Publishing, 2006.

Mount Holly Library. "History of the Langstaff Mansion." http://www.mtholly.lib.nj.us/mansionhistory.html.

Nashua Telegraph. "Hoffman's Detective Arrested; Governor May Refuse to Extradite Ellis Parker." June 4, 1936. http://news.google.com/newspape rs?nid=2209&dat=19360604&id=xRxAAAAAIBAJ&sjid=laQMAAAA IBAJ&pg=6848,4631088.

New Jersey History's Mysteries. http://www.njhm.com/mulliner.htm.

Olsen, Judith Lamb. *Pemberton: An Historic Look at a Village on the Rancocas*. New Orleans, LA: Polyanthos, 1976.

Pennsylvania Haunts and History. http://hauntsandhistory.blogspot.com/2010/04/fort-dix-demons.html.

Pennsylvania State University. Pennsylvania Center for the Book. http://pabook.libraries.psu.edu/palitmap/bios/Roebling__Washington.html.

Peterson, Robert A. *Patriots, Pirates and Pineys: Sixty Who Shaped New Jersey*. Medford, NJ: Plexus Publishing, Inc., 1998.

Philadelphia Inquirer. "Mr. and Mrs. Charles Estill Golden Anniversary." March 9, 1906.

Prison Museum Post 12, no. 1 (May 17, 2012). Official newsletter of the Burlington County Prison Museum Association.

Read, Zachariah. *Dr. Zachariah Read's History of Mount Holly*. N.p., 1859.

Rensselaer Institute Archives and Special Collections. "Roebling Collection, 1830–1926." http://www.lib.rpi.edu/dept/library/html/Archives/access/inventories/pdf%20inventories/MC4_Roebling.pdf.

Revolutionary War New Jersey. "Revolutionary War Sites in Hainesport, New Jersey." http://www.revolutionarywarnewjersey.com/new_jersey_revolutionary_war_sites/towns/hainesport_nj_revolutionary_war_sites.htm.

Riverside Historical Society website. http://riversidenjhistory.org/History.html.

Rizzo, Dennis. *Mount Holly, New Jersey: A Hometown Revisited*. Charleston, SC: The History Press, 2007.

Roebling Museum website. http://roeblingmuseum.org.

Roebling Wire, News from the Roebling Museum, no. 19 (Fall 2013).

Schermerhorn, William. *The History of Burlington, New Jersey*. Burlington, NJ: Press of Enterprise Publishing Co., 1927.

Shreve: The History of an American Family website. http://shrevehistory.com/Places-NJ-Shreveville-Burlington-New-Jersey.xml.

South Jersey Ghost Research. Case notes from investigation of Burlington County Lyceum of History and Natural Sciences, August 2, 2013.

————. Case notes from investigation of Mount Holly Elks, June 30, 2012.

South Jersey Ghost Research website. www.sjgr.org.

South Jersey Paranormal Research website. http://www.sjpr.org.

U.S. Army official website. http://www.army.mil.

Weaber, Gerald. "The Decades Old Mystery of the Watchcase Clock Tower Is Solved." *Gaslight News*, http://rivertonhistory.com/wp-content/uploads/2010/11/134_Gaslight_News_Nov08.pdf.

"Welcome to the Mount Holly Elks Lodge #848." Informational pamphlet compiled by lodge historian Gary Donnelly, PER.

Winzinger, Heidi, personal website. http://www.heidiwinzinger.com/?section=music.

Winzinger, Heidi J., and Mary L. Smith. *Images of America: Mount Holly*. Charleston, SC: Arcadia, 2001.

YouTube. "Ghost Detectives S3EP14 Burlington Library part 1." http://youtu.be/4bnXSfqBIsI.

————. "Ghost Detectives S3EP15 Burlington Library part 2." http://youtu.be/bVZa13n-4KU.

————. Heidi Winzinger Documentaries. *I'll Save That—An Interview with JoAnn Winzinger*. http://www.youtube.com/watch?v=Hg41PDnKh4c&feature=youtu.be.

Zurbrugg Memorial Hospital website. http://www.zurbrugghospital.com.

About the Author

Jan Lynn Bastien is a freelance writer living in Mount Holly, New Jersey, the very haunted county seat of a very haunted county. Upon finding out about the lingering spirits in her hometown, Jan organized popular Mount Holly ghost tours, which led to her first book, *The Ghosts of Mount Holly: A History of Haunted Happenings*. She feels that  the ghosts do a good job of telling people about this unique and history-rich area, but the real reason they hang around is because it is such a great place to be—they just hate to leave!

Visit us at
www.historypress.net
....
This title is also available as an e-book